# TRUSTING
# GOD

## RESTING IN PEACE

BRENDA L FERRY

**WESTBOW**
PRESS®
A DIVISION OF THOMAS NELSON
& ZONDERVAN

WestBow Press books may be ordered through booksellers or by contacting:

WestBow Press
A Division of Thomas Nelson & Zondervan
1663 Liberty Drive
Bloomington, IN 47403
www.westbowpress.com
844-714-3454

ISBN: 979-8-3850-2848-1 (sc)
ISBN: 979-8-3850-2849-8 (e)

Library of Congress Control Number: 2024912905

Print information available on the last page.

WestBow Press rev. date: 08/08/2024

# CONTENTS

# CONTENTS

# PREFACE

This book is for you. I have always secretly wanted to write a book. I have had a story plot in mind for some time and have struggled with the details. One day I was talking to the Lord about it, and I heard Him say in my heart something like, I will let you write this book someday but first, I want you to write about how You have been learning to trust me.

So, here we are, and God says it's time. I can only write about what I know. What I know is that we serve a God who is trustworthy. The truth is, I have spent a lifetime learning this lesson. As gracious as our God is, He is infinitely patient with us and gives us the time we need to get stuff through our thick heads. So, my story may seem long, but it is my hope that I can help you skip a few steps to accelerate your journey towards the same goal, so you can reap the benefits I now enjoy sooner than I have. You see, we all know that there are consequences for our actions. These consequences are known as benefits when we do what's right. My mother said something once that has always stuck with me regarding this. She said that while we will reap consequences for our poor decisions and bad behavior, God, in his mercy, will often 'thin the crop'😊 as we walk towards obedience! I have developed my own philosophy regarding <u>good</u> behavior! I believe that, while we all know that some things will only settle into belief in our hearts through personal experience, the wise person will endeavor to learn from other trusted friends' experiences so that they can skip a few crucial steps to save time getting to the prized goal!! And so, I ask for your patience as I try to help you skip a few steps and accelerate your own journey to trusting a God who loves you and wants desperately to have relationship with you. All He wants is ALL of you. This might seem like a difficult ask but when you consider what He offers you in return, there really is only one intelligent answer. See, He wants ALL of you, but you get ALL of Him in return and it will take an eternity for us to exhaust ALL of who HE is. We ARE talking about the God of the Universe after all. The One who said, "Let there be" and it was done. He is still the Creator and is still actively molding us into His image. All he needs from us is, "YES Lord!"

You see, when we say "Yes," to Him, even when it makes us feel vulnerable or it hurts to let Him stretch us, in the end it is worth it all! Here is the message I feel God has for all of us:

**<u>If you will willingly submit yourself completely to Him and say YES to Him, He Will Expand your Capacity to Fit HIS purposes for your life!</u>**

Our job is to say we trust Him completely. IF we will do this there is absolutely no limit to what God can and will do in and through us. The choice is always ours. He won't force us to do anything we don't want to do. Will we fail at times? Sure. We are human after all. So, what then? We just get up, dust ourselves off and say something like, "Forgive me Lord. Now, where were we again?" and keep moving along the road He is leading us on. You might still be thinking "What's in it for me?" Well, think about it. As God's child, every promise in the Book is yours. You are under His protective umbrella so to speak! Nothing is too difficult for our God who loves to give good gifts to His kids. So, are you ready.

# CHAPTER 1
# **THE BEGINNING**

*13. For you created my inmost being; you knit me together in my mother's womb.*

*14. I praise you because I am fearfully and wonderfully made; your works are wonderful; I know that full well.*

*15. My frame was not hidden from you when I was made in the secret place, when I was woven together in the depths of the earth.*

*16. your eyes saw my unformed body; all the days ordained for me were written in your book before one of them came to be.*

*17. How precious to me are your thoughts, God! How vast is the sum of them!*

> **18. Were I to count them, they would**
> **outnumber the grains of sand — when I**
> **awake, I am still with you!**
> **(Psalms 139:13-18 AMPC)**

I call myself a "wanna be" woodworker! I have all the cool equipment because my husband loves me and wants to buy me all the neat toys to help me in my endeavors to build something "really cool."

One day I was sitting in my best friend's kitchen thinking, *Man, how does she do all that she does with so little counter space*? My friend is an amazing cook who runs a large household. At the time, she had two grown sons and a daughter in high school, not to mention her grandchildren, who were often staying with her, and her best friends who were always showing up at dinner time (that would be me and my husband 😊).

From that day on, a plan began to form in my mind. I was going to build her an island. I had a piece of marble we brought back from Italy that we never use that would work great for the top. Then I began to puzzle out how I would create the frame. I was so excited that it actually kept me up at night because my mind wouldn't stop planning.

When I finally felt confident enough that I could pull this thing off, I presented the idea to my husband, who was all for it, of course. He thinks I can do anything.

Keep in mind that up to this point, I had not 'created' anything. I had a plan, and it was going to be great. My friend was going to love it and it was going to be such a help to her for sure.

I would love to say that it turned out exactly as I

wanted it to but remember, I said I was a "wanna be" woodworker. So, it wasn't perfect, but I put all my love into it, and my friend loved it and uses it all the time.

Now think of the above scripture. God has a plan for everything he creates, and that includes you. The difference is, He is God Almighty, the Master Builder, if you will. He doesn't make mistakes. He has a perfect plan, and he executes it flawlessly. This is true for the day you were created. It didn't start the day you were born. It started much sooner as the Creator put together a plan for your entire life and then began to bring it to reality in your mother's womb.

I believe that one of the enemy's most effective weapons is insecurity. He is cunning in getting us to believe the lie that we aren't worth much. I know he was successful in this tactic with me for many years.

You may be reading this and nodding your head because you feel the same way. If so, please re-read the scripture above. If you believe God's word is true, then that scripture refutes the lie of the enemy that you have no worth.

It says that you are the carefully thought-out creation of God Almighty. He created you like an artist creates his masterpiece. Have you ever wondered, "Why am I like this? Why do I do that?" I realize that as we grow and develop, sin has its input into our lives, but what if God intended for you to be OCD? Or what if God intended for you to have ADHD? Now, He wouldn't call these traits by such names. The enemy of your soul will take what God intended for good and warp it into something negative if he can.

These traits are certainly seen as negative in society but what if God put that inside you to equip you for the work He created for you to do? Perhaps attention to detail is crucial for you.

Perhaps what the world calls ADHD is what God calls energy and drive to accomplish demanding tasks He has set before you. The world sees these traits as negative and wants to medicate them. What if, instead, we saw them as God-given traits and looked for ways to help individuals develop these tendencies in positive and effective practices?

These are just two traits I picked because I am what some might call OCD, or at the very least a perfectionist and my husband has ADHD. So, I am familiar with them and their effect on a person.

Perhaps you are a procrastinator. I can identify with that as well. Again, this is considered a negative trait. However, what if God put that in you to keep you from acting in haste. You take time to think things through. You don't make rash decisions. You think before you speak, etc. These are just a few examples of things I believe God puts in us that he intends to develop and use for His Glory. However, sometimes the devil gets ahold of us, and we start believing his lies. Then we are diverted from our God-given purpose.

What if we were to take our character traits to the Lord and ask Him which ones we need to get rid of and which ones He wants us to develop and use with discipline? Just imagine what God could do in and through us!

If you are that person that truly feels that you are a hopeless cause, I want to challenge you to seek God! He DOES have a purpose for your life! He does want to use you. It might not be as glamorous as you think it should look but God says it is vital to the kingdom!

The point is–we all fit into God's plan. The problem arises when we think our part is too small and doesn't matter because it doesn't look important. Imagine a puzzle of a sunrise. There are many pieces that do not have distinctive markings. It takes the person putting the puzzle together some time to figure out where such a piece fits, but the persistent one doesn't give up. They will set it aside for a while and work on a different area but eventually they will figure it out and place that piece where it fits.

The next time you feel small or insignificant, think about that time you were putting a puzzle together and you put the last loose piece in its spot only to realize that there was still an empty spot. A piece of the puzzle was missing, and the picture could not be completed. Suddenly, that piece that has no distinct markings becomes especially important! You are going to hunt under the couch, get the broom out and do everything you can to find that piece so you can complete your puzzle and hang that beautiful thing on a wall to display your accomplishments.

The moral of this story is, don't let the enemy trick you into being the missing piece of the puzzle!

You may be thinking that this doesn't have much to do with trusting God. It is, however, the true beginning of my story and yours. As my Pastor would say, "That isn't part of my sermon, but it's good advice you can use!"

*And I am convinced and sure of this very thing, that He Who began a good work in you will continue until the day of Jesus Christ [right up to the time of His return] developing [that good work] and perfecting and bringing it to full completion in you. (Philippians 1:6 AMPC)*

# CHAPTER 2
# MY STORY

I say again, my story and yours begins before we were a gleam in our parents' eyes. God had a plan for me before anyone else did. So, God <u>chose</u> me before I was even thought of. The next crucial point in every Christian's life is the day we choose Him!

I was only about 3 ½ years old the day I made that decision for myself. You may think that I was too young for such a decision to count, but I would beg to differ with you. I clearly remember that day and it was definitely the start for me.

As a young girl, I always sat on the left side of the sanctuary near the piano that my mother played.

As always, my mother would play something appropriate during the altar call given at the end of the sermon every service. That particular day the circumstances were decidedly different. That day, I decided to get up from my seat and make my way to the altar. I chose a spot just in front of my mother's piano. My mother did not hesitate once she realized what was happening. She quietly let the music fade and made her way to my side. She took the time to ask me why I was there and made sure I understood what I needed to do. I remember her telling me about the big book Jesus had where He kept all the names of His children for a record. She asked me if I wanted Him to put my name in His book. I said I did, and while I don't remember the exact words, I know she led me in a simple prayer that I could understand, and heaven gained another saint.

As I got older and gained in understanding, there were times that I would reaffirm that decision. And as always, my mother was right there to guide me when needed and leave the rest to the Lord, praying always, I am sure! I am so grateful for my godly mother who didn't care who was uncomfortable with the idea that she stopped playing for everyone else so she could focus on her baby's eternity. Thanks, Mom!!

My earliest memories are of church. My current Pastor teases me about being born in the nursery and I always chuckle at how close to being true that is. I have truly known nothing other than a godly heritage and I am forever grateful for that! My own mother is the hero of my story. In the early days, she was the one who made sure we were up and headed to church whenever the doors were open. My Father, while a Christian, was not a particularly good spiritual leader. I have no memories of him teaching me how to live a godly life. I know he worked in a factory when I was younger. And mom was a schoolteacher in both public and private schools. To me things seemed good in those days.

I was the cute little girl whose long black curly hair all the girls always wanted to play with. Mom participated in whatever my older brother and I were involved in. When I was little, she was the Sunday School leader and taught Children's Church. She played the piano at church for services as I mentioned before. She led the choir, etc. etc. We will get back to Mom for sure but for now let's look at the next step.

## STEPPING INTO POWER

Now, before we go any further, I feel it's time for a heart-to-heart talk. It is my feeling that words like 'denomination' or 'religion' are words that make sad the heart of our heavenly Father! They are words that the enemy of our soul uses to divide us! For the sake of full disclosure, I would like to say here that I consider myself a spirit filled, Bible-believing, tongue-talking Christian who was raised in a full gospel church..... Now, I can almost hear the slap of this book being forcefully closed and the thump as it is thrown on the table. I can even imagine that I hear the loud stomp of retreating feet exiting the room in disgust and I am saddened myself.

If you are still with me, let me say thank you.

Look, I get it. We have a bad reputation of being "out there". Well, that's not God's fault. It is ours. Just as sure as all God's gifts are good, there is just as certainly someone who will take and distort that good thing and mess it up. Of course, there are those among us who have misused the giftings of the Holy Spirit. But if you're honest, you have your "out there" people too, right? Someone who takes a piece of your doctrine to the extreme and messes it up for everyone else.

So maybe it's time to bury the hatchet, so to speak, or at least agree to disagree for the time being.

Let me continue by asking you to assess with me. Do you believe that the Bible is the inspired word of God? If the answer is yes, then we are on the right track, I believe! I do not claim to know everything, and I certainly would expect you to verify the truth or lack thereof, held in the pages of this book. For me, the standard is the Word of God. It doesn't matter whether you believe in the Baptism of the Holy Spirit or not. Unless you can show me in scripture where it says that this is not for me, then I would respectfully disagree with your assessment. Besides, As I have said earlier, there is no arguing with experience. I have experienced this, and you will never convince me otherwise!

I once had a conversation with someone who did not share my 'denomination' nor my convictions in this area. She believed that speaking in tongues was something of the enemy. While she never said as much, I think she actually thought that people who claimed to have been baptized with the Holy Spirit with the evidence of speaking in other tongues were demon-possessed. I told her that all I knew was that God was a good God who wanted to give good gifts to his children.

There is no doubt that when you give your heart to God, the Holy Spirit becomes a part of you. That is scriptural. So, if that is all there is, why did God tell his disciples, who already called him Lord, to go and wait in the upper room for the Comforter, Who, by the way, is called the Spirit of Truth in John 14:16,17.

*But Ye shall receive power (ability and might) when the Holy Spirit has come upon you, and you shall be my witnesses in Jerusalem and all Judea and Samaria and to the ends (the very bounds) of the earth.*
*Acts 1:8 (AMPC)*

The disciples obeyed and were filled with the Holy Spirit and spoke in unknown tongues. I don't find anything that says that this was ever done away with. So, I challenged her to open herself up to an Almighty God and ask Him if this were something He would like her to have, and if so, be willing to receive. Her response still makes me a little angry! She gasped and said, "Oh, NO, I could never do that. That would open the door for the devil to come in and cause me no end of trouble!" I was so angry with her!! How dare she say that my Loving Father would allow something like that to happen when I come to Him with complete trust, open and ready to receive all His goodness. As if the enemy could sneak past an Almighty God. Really??

Okay, let me take a breath and say, I offer you the same challenge! God is a good Father!! The scripture talks about that, right. He's not going to give you a stone if you ask for a piece of bread.

You might be surprised by His response!! Again, the Lord is a gentleman and will not force anything on you. Note that I didn't ask you to drop your 'label' nor do I offer to drop mine, as it is. Can we proceed simply as fellow Christians exploring all of whom God is, prepared to be surprised by the goodness we may find along the way? I can testify that during my relationship with God, I have been both humbled and surprised by His amazing love and care for me! I have felt so undeserving and yet He is so tender and careful with us as His kids. He reminds me often that He knows me better than I know myself. I can trust Him, for He is trustworthy!

Let me just say here that as a child of God, I want every good gift God has. I understand that I can sometimes get in the way of God giving me good things. Remember, sin separates us from God. So, before I go on, let me share a practice that I have that you might consider adopting. I make it a habit to go before God with the following Scripture:

> *Search me [thoroughly], O God, and know*
> *my heart! Try me and know my thoughts!*
> *And see if there is any wicked or hurtful way*
> *in me and lead me in the way everlasting.*
> *Psalms 139:23,24 (AMPC)*

If you genuinely want to learn to trust God more, this is a good practice to start! I will say, don't pray that prayer if you aren't prepared to make difficult changes in your life.

Remember, you can't trust someone you don't know. You must build a relationship with someone before you can trust them. This is a wonderful way to build a relationship with the Lord. I promise you He will answer the honest heart of anyone who cries out to Him with a prayer such as this!

Okay, if you are still with me, let's proceed, shall we?

The next, important, step in my journey was, indeed, the baptism of the Holy Spirit. Ironically, I honestly do not remember how old I was or any of the particulars of the actual event. So, I am unable to give you any delicious detail, as it were. I recently discussed this with my mother. She wasn't completely sure, but she says that she thought she remembered me speaking in a heavenly language at the time I gave my heart to God. Perhaps she is right. Again, I do not recall myself. I do know that I received what we would, in our circles, call a re-filling of the Holy Spirit when I was a little older, about 8 years old. Again, I don't really remember the specifics. What I do remember, however, is the difference I noticed in myself. I remember thinking how different I felt. I was stronger, somehow. I even imagined I was more 'mature' than before which any young girl would fancy, I suppose. It was more of a confidence I felt, that wasn't there before. Anyway, I felt something way down deep in what my Pastor calls my 'knower' that I had taken a significant step closer to God and I was pleased with the difference!

I want to take time here to implore you not to take for granted the power and the ministry of the Holy Spirit. When Christ Jesus left this earth, he told his disciples to go into an upper room and wait for the Comforter to come. He told the disciples that the Holy Spirit would guide them into all truth. Wow, how many times have you longed to know the truth of a matter. It has been my experience that the Holy Spirit is a wonderful companion if we pay attention!

Have you ever had a bad feeling about something? Perhaps you forged ahead only to regret your decision. I would submit that that 'bad feeling' was the Holy Spirit of God trying to warn you away from something harmful to you. Often, He works like this, I believe. Sometimes, it's something much more practical. A good example is the day I was in my favorite place, my kitchen, happily making one of my favorite recipes, pumpkin bread. I was just about to pour the batter into the pans when I had the thought, "You better taste that first." For once, I paid attention and was horrified to find that I had obviously left out the salt. I could almost picture the Holy Spirit tapping me on the shoulder and whispering such a warning. Since then, I have too often ignored such warnings and have experienced much frustration because of it.

I said all that to say that if you will pay attention, the Holy Spirit, who was sent as our "Helper" will help you in ways you could never imagine. The next time you have what I often call a rogue thought, don't ignore it. It might just be the Holy Spirit trying to help you avoid some small grief. It may be small but, on such things, does the Peace of God that we enjoy often depend!!

Don't ignore the person of the Holy Spirit!! He is the third part of the Trinity, and as such, He is God. Talk to Him and ask Him to guide you throughout your day. Then try to pay close attention to any so-called rogue thoughts and obey their dictates and see if you don't begin to experience more peace and confidence. I, for one, am still learning and miss the mark often. When I do, I recognize my mistake, ask forgiveness, and charge on to the next opportunity to get it right!

Now perhaps we are prepared to hear a little about my spiritual heritage before I take you through some of the other steps in my journey.

But first, I would like to start a practice at the end of each chapter throughout the rest of this book. I believe it's especially important to set good habits and make positive declarations. So, I would like to start with this verbal declaration at the end of each of the following chapters. If you can say Amen, please join me by saying the following out loud:

**<u>"God, I believe that You are who You say You are and that You'll do what You say You'll do! I choose to put my complete trust in You. You are my hope and my salvation!</u>**

**<u>Today I say YES to You, Jesus!"</u>**

## CHAPTER 3

# GRANDMA O'BRIAN

My Grandmother on my mom's side of the family was a special lady!! Grandma O'Brian was a bit of a mystery to me growing up. I wish I had known her better, but I did have the privilege of being around her a lot, as we lived with her for a time, and later, we lived next door to her and grandpa. Even then I am ashamed to say that I didn't know them as well as I should have. If you are young and still have your grandparents in your life, I would challenge you to take time to get to know them! Ask them questions about their lives when they were younger! Draw all you can from their wells of wisdom! They have lived life and have much wisdom to share. Perhaps they can even help you skip a few steps themselves! Just sayin'! Don't stop with your grandparents. You know those little old ladies at church that you ignore? I would dare you to sit next to them and get them talking about their experiences. I promise you they are a well of wisdom worth drawing from! Perhaps, in doing so, you might bring a breath of fresh air to their lives as well. You will not regret it!

I remember Grandma talking about seeing angels and having visions. You can imagine as a young person, this seemed "out there". The truth is she did indeed see angels and seemed to have a unique relationship with the Lord. My mother tells the story of the day she had been outside working in the garden when Grandma, who had been inside having her prayer time, came outside looking very pale and shaky. When Mom asked her what was wrong, she said she had just had a visit from an Angel of the Lord. She said he told her that something had happened that would be very upsetting, but the Lord wanted her to know that it was going to be okay. It was a day or two later when word came that the Pastor of our church had been found drowned in the Lake. He was a good man of God who had shepherded our church well for many years. Hearing this story as an adult, all I can say is WOW! God must have had a special love for my grandmother to send her an angel for comfort. You might say, as I have, why can't I see angels? Good question. Perhaps we would panic or otherwise be unable to handle such an encounter. All I know is that's cool!

I personally can recall a time when my brother and another young man who was a friend of the family and myself were taking a trip to Colorado. In the days leading up to our trip there had been a murder in the parking lot of our shopping mall. This was big news for such a small community. I remember it being the topic of many conversations ending with "What is our world coming to!"

So, we headed out and had a wonderful time visiting our friend's sister and experiencing the beauty of the Colorado Mountains. It was a great trip.

When I arrived home, I was met by an incredibly grateful Grandma. She said she was so happy that we were home safe. It seems that while we were gone, the Lord gave her a vision of our car driving down the road. She could see only one person who she felt must be me driving. She also sensed that evil was following me. Later she said she was convinced that the person following me was the very man who had committed the murder everyone was talking about. She got busy praying for me and in her vision, two heads popped up from the back seat, my brother and friend, I presume, who had been sleeping. When the person following saw this they veered away, and the burden of prayer lifted from my grandmother's heart. She was an intercessor and I, for one, am grateful for her services!

The following is a story that my uncle relates about what it was like to have a praying mother. These are his words:

> *It was after I graduated from high school, and I had a very good friend who was definitely not a Christian. He was a couple years older than I was, but he was a great guy. He would give you the shirt off his back if you needed it. After I graduated, I moved to Cedar Rapids and my friend, John, and I eventually ended up moving into an apartment together. I left it up to him to find one because I was working full time and he was a tree trimmer so when it rained, he couldn't work. Anyway, he told*

me he had found a place, so he took me down to the 16ᵗʰ avenue Tap on the corner. It was a two-story building, and the upper story had a one-bedroom apartment in it. It was dirt cheap because it was over the tavern and could be loud. So, we secured it and moved in, and we were just as happy as a meadowlark. I gave him the bedroom for obvious reasons, and I took the couch. Anyway, a couple three weeks into it on a Saturday night, I had been out with my girlfriend and came back at about 1:30 AM. I came up the stairs quietly because my roommate had company. So, I went in, making as little noise as possible, and headed to my couch and got my blanket and my pillow. I was getting laid down all nice and comfortable. There was a streetlight on the corner, and we never pulled a shade or anything because that streetlight shown in the room, and we would walk around in there like it was daylight. So, we saved money like that, see (chuckle, chuckle 😊). Anyway, I had gotten all nice and comfortable, and all wound up in the blanket. I must have dozed off because something woke me up a little bit and I opened my eyes and the first thing I saw was the silhouette of a person standing behind me. That person had something in their hand. I was frozen in fear with hair standing on the back of my head and the whole works. Then a deep voice says, " I am going to finish you once and for all". At that point John wakes up *because they had spoken rather loudly. The person had a knife in his hand and was getting ready to jab me in the back. My roommate says, "Hey, what are you doing?" Those weren't his exact words but something like that. Then the guy turned around and dove right at John. Then I thought, oh great, now I got John in trouble. But instead of trying to stab John, he smacked him in the jaw and went right on by him and down the stairs and he was gone. That, of course, woke everybody up so I got up and made coffee. This was 2 or 3 in the morning. We were young and could drink coffee any time day or night. It didn't seem to bother us at all. Anyway, we were sitting there discussing the whole thing and the telephone rang. John looked at me and I looked at him and, of course, this was way before cell phones.*

*John says, "I'll get it, I think." He had those great big eyes of his wide as he went and picked up the phone. He said 'hello?', dead silence. Finally, he puts the phone out and says, "it's your mother?!"!*

*I said "really?". So, I took the phone and said "Mom?"*

*"Yes Donnie, it's me. The Lord just woke me up out of a dead sleep and told me to get down on my hands and knees and pray for you because you were in trouble. Are you okay?"*

I said "Mom, you have no idea how glad I am to hear your voice! Yes, I was in trouble, but I am okay now. Evidently the Lord was saving me through you".

Then she says "AMEN" and she started speaking in tongues. Then, of course, I couldn't understand anything so I told her to call me when she could speak English (more chuckling). We talked about it later and Mom says it was just as plain as day. God told her "Your youngest is in trouble. Get up and pray for him now." Thank God she was a prayer warrior.

Another time, Dad had an old Buick that I had knocked the transmission out of it. I felt guilty about it. It had been sitting out there in the weeds and I took it upon myself. I was going to jack that thing up and pull the transmission out and put a good one in it for him. I had the thing jacked up in a very precarious way. The jack was sinking into the mud, and it was hotter than blazes.

Then Mom comes out with the neighborhood kids all around her and hollers "Donnie, where you at?".

I said, "I'm under the car, Ma."

She says, "Get out of there!"

*"What's going on?", I asked.*

*"Just get out of there!" and I thought, well, she must need me for something. So, I got out and my head just cleared the door jamb when the jack gave way and it dropped. I would have been right under the middle of it.*

*"Thank you, Jesus!", that's all she says-and then, her with three little kids surrounding her, she hollers, "I'll race you back to the house." The Lord had told her to come and get me.*

*Those are just a couple of stories. There are many things that I am certain I do not know about because she was faithful to pray me out of stuff and I didn't even realize. That's why prayer is so important.*

These are just a few examples of the heritage I have from my grandmother. Oddly, I haven't seen any angels nor has my mother that I know of. However, the Lord has taught us through her example that He is a good God who loves His children and works with us in real and personal ways. The way he worked through her was specific to her personality and gifting. The same with my mother. As I have said, my mother is my spiritual hero. Her relationship with God, however, is different than was my grandmother's. For all her spiritual prowess, my grandmother was a worrier. I have a tough time wrapping my mind around that, given all the stories I have heard about her. I do remember my mother making the statement that she was determined NOT to be a worry wart, like Grandma always had been. So, God used her, as the next generation, to teach me what she had learned about refusing to worry about things that were out of her control anyway and simply trust God. Sadly, as good of an example as she presented before my brother and me, it still took me too long to learn this lesson. We can sure be thick-headed sometimes!

As I write this, I can imagine that there is at least one person out there reading this that is thinking something like, "Well, that's really nice for you, but I have no such spiritual heritage to build on." I want to encourage you with a reminder that God is an individual God. He is a gentleman and will not force you to do anything that you choose not to do. That means that the people in your history could and perhaps have chosen not to follow the Lord. That does not mean that there is no hope for you. I have told you before that God loves you and wants relationship with you. The choice is always yours. Recently I had the privilege of hearing the testimony of a young lady from our church that was telling her story as part of our recovery program. As I sat and listened to her talk about living on the street-no home, no support structure at all-I was moved to tears. After the service I told her how proud I was of her for having the courage to share her story with us. I also told her that I felt like a spiritual snob compared to the nightmare she had experienced. As I thought on it later, I realized that there is no limit to the extent to which God will chase after us, waiting for us to choose Him as He has already chosen us. Just like He has watched over me all my life, He had watched over this young lady and kept her from serious harm while He pursued her until she finally yielded her life to Him and allowed Him to transform her into the beautiful young woman of God that she is today. That's how much my God loves me and you!!!

Don't ever think that you are a lost cause!! There is no circumstance or anyone, beyond God's reach!! It only takes a consistent "yes" from you to see your life transformed. Since we are talking about trusting God, let me say that I am not just talking to those who do not know the Lord. Perhaps you have been a Christian all your life but live in a constant state of anxiety. Let me say to you, God does NOT wish for you to continue in such a state!! You can have perfect peace if you choose to! You might have to do some fighting to get it and practice vigilance to keep it. However, it can be done!!

How do you do it? It starts with a choice. Just like our mantra. You must decide if you believe God is who He says He is and that He will do what He says He will do. Then you must make a conscious choice to trust him with whatever the current situation is that is trying to steal your peace and joy. I have said it before and I will keep saying it, say it out loud "Lord, I trust you with _____!!" Then make a conscience choice to refuse to worry about it!! Often when I am battling the temptation to worry about something, I will have to stop myself multiple times throughout a day and speak out loud such words as I have suggested. I usually add a plea for forgiveness to the Lord for worrying in the first place!! This kind of struggle may take a couple days before I start to feel that wonderful peace I mentioned, but it does come, and I am forever grateful for my wonderful, patient, Heavenly Father who continues to be faithful to me even when I am often so fragile as to need His help multiple times over the same issue.

I am determined to be like David, who "encouraged himself in the Lord." I can imagine him having conversations with himself where he is reminding himself that he does believe in the power of an Almighty God who loves him and is more than able to take care of him. I want to grow up to be just like David in this respect. David was a worshipper who was far from perfect, but he didn't give up. He would mess up, repent, dust himself off and forge ahead with the Lord. I think we could all learn from his example!

Let me end this chapter by saying that I want to grow up to be a woman of prayer like my grandmother. I want to be found faithfully standing in the gap for others!

Oh Lord that I might be found faithful to stand in that gap!

*The Earnest (heartfelt, continued) [prayer of a righteous man makes tremendous power available {dynamic in its working}.*
*James 5:16b (AMPC)*

*And I sought a man among them who should build up the wall and stand in the gap before Me for the land, that I should not destroy it, but I found none, Ezekiel 22:30 (AMPC)*

25

Ready for our declaration?

**<u>"God, I believe that You are who You say You are and that You'll do what You say You'll do! I choose to put my complete trust in You. You are my hope and my salvation!</u>**

**<u>Today I say YES to You, Jesus!"</u>**

# CHAPTER 4
# MOM

Now we can focus on my mother again. As I have already said, she has always been my Spiritual hero and has become my closest friend! I don't reckon this ever happens until your children become mature adults with children of their own. In order to be a good parent, you will often have to choose discipline and correction over friendship when your children are young. When they are adults and you do not have the same control, there is room to develop friendship with your kids. I often hang my head in shame when I realize all the grief I caused my mother as a young girl, not to mention all the things I took for granted, not realizing or even really thinking about how hard life was for her.

You see, my mom married my father, who was the youngest of ten kids. I honestly don't know that much about her earlier years before us kids came along but I can surmise that it wasn't always easy.

As I said, she has always been the one who pointed us to Jesus. She was our solid foundation. She got us to church, and somehow, made birthdays and Christmas special on a super tight budget. We wanted for nothing, truly. We were secure in the knowledge that we were loved and that she would always be there for us. I realize now that she sheltered us a lot from issues with my father. Here I will simply say that my memories of my father were good early on. I was his favorite and could do no wrong, which was cool when I was little. Later, when he quit a perfectly good job to pursue his dream as an artist and started making jewelry out of silverware, I began to realize that all was not well in paradise. He would travel to flea markets, etc., and I would often go with him on the weekends. You can imagine that this didn't pay nearly as well as the steady job he quit. So, the burden was laid heavier on my mother's shoulders to make ends meet. That said, my father was truly talented and did fairly well for a couple of years and then simply quit everything. Then my memories became of him sleeping and eating a lot and hollering at us kids to be quiet, because he was trying to rest. And the burden got heavier.

Never a word of complaint did my mother utter within my hearing. I don't know who she talked to except God. I knew she talked to Him for sure!! No doubt about that!! Here is a funny story to emphasize how smart and strong she was: Once when I was dating a delinquent, for real, when we started dating, he had just gotten out of Juvie for breaking into parking meters. I let him drive the car even though he didn't have a license. I wanted to enjoy sitting beside him with his arm around me. I knew it was wrong, and my guilty conscience finally got the best of me. After about a month or so, I confessed my sin to my mother. In her wisdom she said something like, "Yes, I know. God talks to me all the time when I am in prayer but thank you for telling me." 😊 Is she smart or what?? I always thought twice before doing anything foolish, knowing God would tell on me.

I can remember many times when I would come home from work late in the evening or in the wee hours of the morning and see her light click off as I pulled into the driveway.

Mom loved kids! Especially the awkward young teenage crowd, she says they are her favorite. She would take in stray animals and stray kids with equal enthusiasm! Multiple times we took young men into our home. I remember Joey and David to name a couple. These guys became like big brothers to me. Mom would feed them and love on them and point them to Jesus just like she did us while, never neglecting us. We never felt slighted at all.

Then came the time when I was 11 years old and Dad had gone to Southern Iowa, which is where his family was. I still don't know all the circumstances, and they are not important for our purposes. Suffice it to say, that the Lord finally gave my mom release to divorce my father, when he wrote home and asked her to send him some clothes. Before this, I remember a particular incident where Dad had yelled at my big brother and called him irresponsible and had made him cry. I was devastated because, as I have said, my brother was my hero, so I ran to my room crying. That day I grew up just a little and wouldn't have anything to do with Dad trying to make up with me. I finally understood that being "Daddy's little girl" wasn't all it was cut out to be.

So, Dad left, and we ended up moving in with my grandparents in town, and life went on.

Being a teacher, my mom had the summers off, so she planted three large gardens. It was a lot of work but helped make ends meet. Again, I never heard a word of complaint from my mother. That was my department, I am ashamed to say! Mom, she just kept moving forward, her eyes on the Lord. Now I can only shake my head and marvel at her strength of commitment and her courage, not to mention, I now realize, her strong determination to Trust her God!

I have a love of music and singing that I inherited from my mother. This she nurtured in me over the years. I mentioned that she was the choir director. I also mentioned that she was always at church early, so guess who else was there? So naturally, I sang in the choir. I started as an alto and later a soprano. My mother, being an English major would pick out a Cantata and then write a "screen play" of sorts to go with it. Those were some awesome days. Oh yeah, she also did this for the private school we attended, and where she taught as well. Now I wonder what she did in her "spare time." Seems to me there couldn't have been much of that.

There was a stretch where we went to public school. During that time, my brother learned to play the trombone and I the Clarinet, and you guessed it, Mom convinced us both to play for church. So, we had a little family band going. This served to give me confidence to use my gifts for God's glory.

Mom had spiritual gifts that sometimes scared me, as

I have said. She often gave a word of interpretation after a message in tongues was given or would give a word of prophecy.

She took time to teach me about the gift of discernment and the word of knowledge. Like the time we were headed home after service, and she was driving. I remember thinking, "Man, she is really going fast. She should slow down". The thought had no sooner gone through my head than there were flashing lights behind us, and we were being pulled over. Sure enough, mom got a speeding ticket (Sorry, Mom, didn't mean to rat you out 😊). After the police officer was gone, I made the mistake of telling her my thoughts right before she got pulled over. She reprimanded me gently and told me that this was the word of knowledge, and would I please be so kind as to share these thoughts in the future <u>before</u> she gets pulled over.

Or what about the time when my mother was in the hospital in traction because of back problems. My big brother had taken me to church, as I was too young to have a driver's license. One of my favorite things was to go warm up the car. On this occasion I was sitting in the car just outside the door that most people used to come in and out of church. I was feeling quite grown up and then suddenly, I had this fear come over me. I had a strong urge to get out of that car and get inside the church quickly. As I did so, I remember hearing what sounded like a foot scuff behind me which prompted me to run inside. I couldn't have been gone for more than just a minute or two as I went inside and told my brother I was cold and ready to go. When we got back to the parking lot the car was gone. When I told my mother this story, she thanked God for protecting me and said that that feeling of fear that I had was the Holy Spirit telling me to run to safety because He knew what I didn't. She was glad that I had listened. Otherwise perhaps I would have gone with the car, and it may not have ended well for me.

I have said before that Mom never complained. She also made a point to never bad mouth my father after the divorce. I never heard her talk bad about him. The fact is, she never complained about anyone or anything to any extent that I can remember. I marvel again at her strength of character, or was it perhaps that she learned early how to trust in God and rest in that trust? I think perhaps a little of both.

When I became a wife and mother myself, Mom always had time to listen to me fuss. I am afraid I took after our worry-wart grandmother rather than my uncomplaining mother in this regard. She would listen to me fuss and sometimes give me a word from the Lord but mostly she just kept pointing me to God. I remember always being challenged and uncomfortable at times. She would give me her best advice, and I would think, "Yeah, right, I am not doing that." Her advice was good, but my courage was not up to the task. Yet she never lowered her standards or agreed with me when I complained that my husband wasn't doing right. She would just encourage me to love him and keep praying and putting my trust in God.

The grandkids came and mom made her trips to wherever we were. She was determined not to miss out on their lives. We always went home at least once a year, and we could depend on her to come our way once a year as well. She even came to Italy when we were stationed there. You will hear more about that later. So, my kids got to know her well. When they were old enough, they each got to spend a summer with her. She invested in them heavily just like she does with anyone who crosses her path. I mentioned that she was an English teacher. Did I mention that she has a gift when it comes to storytelling? My kids grew up with "Grandma's stories" on cassette tape. Any given night you could hear her voice coming from all three of my kids' rooms as they fell asleep to her stories. You guessed it, each story was uplifting and pointed them to Jesus. At this writing, my mother is truly my best friend and all-time spiritual hero! We talk often and share prayer requests. She has taught me the importance of prayer. She is 87 years old and has macular degeneration. This has left her home-bound and unable to cook extensively like she wants to, another passion she passed down to me. While she is unable to drive and often needs assistance because of her sight issues, she amazes me with how much she can accomplish! I am especially impressed with how she still actively seeks God for purpose in her life. She leads a prayer group once a week, teaching others how to connect with God. She has folks who come to her house to be mentored. She is still taking in folks who need a place to rest their heads. Meanwhile she feeds them good with natural and Spiritual foods.

She spends every morning in prayer after she gets my brother and nephew off to work. She takes good care of her physical health by resting every afternoon and spends the evening listening to her favorite YouTube preachers or Christian programs. I know every family member's name as well as her spiritual children's names are mentioned in prayer every week. I often wonder who will fill the shoes of our seniors when they are gone. It seems that God has chosen me to be that person for mom. I will tell you more about that later. I have spent a bit of time here with my mom's story for a very good reason. She has been a shining example to me all my life. She exemplifies what it means to live a lifestyle of trusting God and still it has taken me way too long to "get it". Again, it is my hope to accelerate your journey to where you get to enjoy the God-intended benefit of trusting Him sooner than I did in life!

*Whatever may be your task, work at it heartily (from the soul), as [something done] for the Lord and not for men, Knowing [with all certainty] that it is from the Lord [and not from men] that you will receive the inheritance which is your [real] reward. [The One Whom] you are actually serving [is] the Lord Christ (the Mesiah).*
*Colossians 3:23,24 (AMPC)*

Ready for our declaration?

**"God, I believe that You are who You say You are and that You'll do what You say You'll do! I choose to put my complete trust in You. You are my hope and my salvation!**

**Today I say YES to You, Jesus!**

## CHAPTER 5

# THE CHURCH

Before we go any further, I want to mention the church I grew up in. It is a part of my Spiritual heritage that bears mentioning!

I attended the same Foursquare Gospel Church until I married and moved away. One of my favorite memories is of the first Pastor I ever knew. His name was Pastor Griffis. I am sure he had a first name but to me he was always Pastor Griffis. He was a very stern man. I only remember one sermon that he preached because it caught my attention so strongly. He talked about getting your "want to" fixed. That message has followed me to this day. I mean, don't we all desire things that we shouldn't? When you want something, that desire drives you. If I want things that are not good for me, my natural self will do whatever it takes to get them. This is a problem that I dare say plagues all of humanity. It started with Eve and has carried on through the ages. To combat this natural tendency, we must allow the Spirit to guide us and help us to be big enough to allow the Lord to give us an attitude adjustment when needed. It's part of saying "yes" to Jesus that allows us to keep our "want to" in line. This is a good place to apply Psalms 139: 23,24 mentioned earlier! I have made it a habit to pray this prayer. Then I must follow through when He points out that my "want to" is out of line and ask the Lord to help me fix it! I know that I want to desire Him and what He wants for me more than anything else.

Pastor Griffis' favorite song was "What a Friend We Have in Jesus". I must say that he did NOT have a singing voice, but he would often sing that song as a solo because He loved it so. I dare say he cherished the friendship he had with Jesus. Just think about the lyrics to this song:

### *What a Friend*

*What a friend we have in Jesus —*
*All our sins and griefs to bear*
*What a privilege to carry — everything to God in prayer*
*Oh, what peace we often forfeit —*
*Oh what needless pain we bear*
*All because we do not carry — everything to God in prayer.*

*Have you trials and temptations — is there trouble everywhere?*
*We should never be discouraged — Take it to the Lord in prayer.*
*Can we find a friend so faithful —*
*Who will all our sorrows bear?*
*Jesus knows our every weakness —*
*Take it to the Lord in prayer.*

*Are we weak and heavy laden — cumbered with a load of care?*
*Precious savior, still our refuge — Take it to the Lord in prayer.*
*Do they friends despise, forsake thee?*
*Take it to the Lord in prayer.*
*In His harms He'll take and shield thee —*
*Thou wilt find a solace there.*

As I listened to this stern old man sing this song off key, my respect for him grew. I could see his passionate love for the Lord, and it made me want to have that kind of relationship with the Lord too.

I was reminiscing about this particular memory with my mother, and she told me "The rest of the story" that I had not heard. It seems that this same strong man of God experienced a parent's worst nightmare and survived by holding the hand of his friend Jesus. You see, when he was a young father with little children, he accidentally killed his own child. All mom remembered was that he ran over the child with his vehicle. I mean, WOW! Can any of us even imagine the anguish? How he could survive such an occurrence can only be explained by his relationship with his Jesus. I dare say that no earthly friend or counselor could possibly help someone walk through such a nightmare unless God was filling in the holes that counsel without God would have. When my mom told me that story, my respect for my first pastor grew exponentially. He was truly a man of a mighty God who hung on for dear life and survived. Thank God for his example!

When he called me out by name during a sermon

with a "Brenda Douthart, I am sure that whatever you are digging for in your purse isn't near as important as you paying attention to the Word of God being preached," I was able to receive that because I respected him. You can well imagine I got "the look" from my mother that said I had better get up and come sit by her or she was coming to get me 😊.

I can remember many late-night services where folks would "tarry" at the altar. I can remember my grandmother laughing in the Spirit. You can scoff if you want to, but I was there, and she wasn't giggling with her friends. She was in the presence of the Lord.

I know we shudder at the idea of being at church late but somehow, we survived, and I dare say we thrived!!

I came to understand that spending time in the presence of the Lord was life changing!! You cannot spend time in the presence of God and not be positively affected!!

For myself, I can say that I hunger for more time in His presence so that He can affect change in me. This doesn't have to happen just at church, at the altar. It should be happening at home during our personal time with the Lord. The problem is this takes time and effort that we don't want to spend. Oh, Lord, help us to hunger so deeply for more of You that we are willing to give You our time and energy freely and let You have your way with us!

God is so holy, there is no way we could possibly handle all of who He is at one time. I am sure that is why positive changes in us take time. If God loaded us up with all His Glory, we would certainly die. Think about the priests in the Old Testament who couldn't stand because the presence of the Lord was so heavy. That reminds me of another favorite scripture:

> *And all of us, as with unveiled faces, [because we]*
> *continued to behold [in the Word of God] as in a*
> *mirror the glory of the Lord, are constantly being*
> *transformed into His very own image in ever increasing*
> *splendor and from one degree of glory to another;*
> *[for this comes] from the Lord [who is] the Spirit.*
> *2 Corinthians 3:18 (AMPC)*

So, we can conclude that if we want to be more like Jesus, we need only "get under the spout where the glory comes out" as they say. It's been said that if you hang around with someone long enough you will start acting like them. I have even heard that married couples start looking more alike the longer they are married. The same principle applies here. The more we hang out with the Lord and allow Him to pour His goodness into us, the more like Him we will become. People might even see His likeness in you. All I can say is, "Let it be Lord!"

> *For a day in your courts is better than a thousand*
> *[anywhere else]; I would rather be a door keeper*
> *and stand at the threshold in the house of my God*
> *than to dwell [at ease] in the tents of wickedness.*
> *Psalms 84:20 (AMPC)*

Ready for our declaration?

**<u>"God, I believe that You are who You say You are and that You'll do what You say You'll do! I choose to put my complete trust in You. You are my hope and my salvation!</u>**

**<u>Today I say YES to You, Jesus!</u>**

# CHAPTER 6

# WHO ARE YOU FOLLOWING?

I believe there comes a time in every Christian's life when they must come to terms with why they are serving God. Naturally, a young person will model their life after someone that they admire and trust. For me that was my mother and my big brother especially. I felt like, if my mom said it, it was gospel. If my mom modeled it, then it would be OK.

And I sure believed that if my big brother did it then it was OK. I have come to realize that this just isn't true. We cannot live our lives modeling our Christianity after another person. Not only is it not right, but it's also not safe. The simple truth is a person will let you down eventually simply because they're human and they will make mistakes that will hurt you however unintended it might be. If you grow up thinking a certain person can do no wrong, you will be led astray, because they will do wrong. It's just part of life.

One of my favorite evangelists has a quote that I think of often, in this regard. When he came to the church, I was always excited because I enjoyed his preaching, and he was good-looking and charismatic. He was a great singer. These are all definite attributes to be admired. One time when he came to visit, he said these words: "There are no mighty men or women of God; there are only men and women of a mighty God."

You see, the only person we really should be following is God himself. Our standard should be His Word and His Word only. We need to guard our heart against being offended by our heroes <u>when</u> they make a mistake, which they will. It's our job to support them and pray for them, especially our pastors and teachers. My pastor is someone that I respect more than I can say, and I am committed to praying for him and giving him the grace he needs if he says something that doesn't quite agree with my way of thinking or falls short of my expectations somehow. He is certainly a man of a mighty God whose heart is stayed on Christ, and I know that he would never lead me astray on purpose. Besides, it is highly possible that it is my way of thinking or expectations that might need adjusting, right?

My aim in this chapter is to encourage you to determine where you stand and who you follow, to stand on your own two spiritual feet, so to speak, and, to predetermine how you will react when one of your spiritual heroes fails in some way. Search the scriptures to find out what is your proper response and determine if and/or when the time comes, you will respond appropriately. You see, I wanted to follow my big brother because he was my hero! After my parents divorced when I was eleven, my brother became a father figure to me whether he chose to or not. While I am sure my mother taught me how to drive, Brent was involved in that venture as well. I know he taught me how to play basketball. To say I idolized this poor guy is an understatement. I had him on such a high pedestal that if he failed to live up to this unrealistic image, great and devastating would be the fall!

I do think Brent tried to fill in the empty spots for me. Once, when he took me to the movies, I can remember swelling up with pride, as I foolishly thought, "All these people think I am his date."

He had a 1964 Buick that had a souped-up engine in it. I could hardly wait until I was old enough so I could drive it. Turned out, he blew the engine before I got the chance.

Sometimes, Brent would take me along when he was with his friends. I recall a time when we ran out of gas one evening after dark and he and his friend left me in the car while they went for help. I don't recall why they made that decision, but I am sure it made sense at the time. Anyway, I was so scared but too proud to say anything. They got the help we needed, and all was well in the end.

Even when I became an adult and moved away from home, he continued to be my hero. Once he rode his motorcycle hundreds of miles from Iowa to Florida to visit me when my husband was out to sea. I will never forget the pride I felt when he offered to let me ride his motorcycle. I mean, he handed me the keys and said, "Want to take her for a spin?" The beginning of my marriage started with me mastering the art of operating a motorcycle, and while he had not witnessed this, he was willing to allow me to ride his bike, WHAT?!?! I was so excited that I took longer than I should have, and he got worried. I still chuckle about that today.

My point is Brent tried his best to fill in the empty spots and I still look up to him. Today, he is a father and a grandfather, not to mention a leader in his Church. He has come full circle. Both of my sons moved to Iowa and Uncle Brent has been a big part of their lives. He has invested a lot in Patrick's life especially. Patrick came to Iowa with a desire to learn to hunt. Uncle Brent took him under his wing and taught him to respect guns and operate and care for them responsibly as well as taking him hunting.

Overall, he did well. However, there was a space of time back in the day when he fell away from the Lord. I found out that he was human after all. I was forced to realize that just because my big brother did it, didn't make it OK. That was a tough time for me because I loved him fiercely. I would hear things and shake my head refusing to believe anything negative about my big brother. I now realize that I was placing way too much weight on his shoulders. Forgetting that he had his own struggles to deal with.

That started a journey for me in seeking God to understand what I believed. Of course, my mother always encouraged me to read the Word and to pray and talk to Jesus daily. I confess as a young girl I didn't always do this as consistently as I should, but I did get into the Word, and I did pray, and I did begin to understand and recognize the truth of God's Word for myself.

Perhaps you have been following a person or a particular ministry and haven't really settled on what you believe in for yourself. I would like to caution you strongly here. Do not follow man! Find out what the Word of God says and what you believe and why you believe it. Memorize scripture that pertains to your particular issues as they come. The Bible says His Word will not return void. When you are facing the worst trial of your life God's Word will come up to encourage you, I can testify to that!

So, who do you follow man or God? This is just one more thing you need to decide on your journey towards trusting God. People will fail you because they are imperfect beings that, no matter how hard they try, will not always hit the mark. God, on the other hand, is perfect and cannot fail. Also, He never changes His mind. He is the same yesterday, today and forever (Hebrews 13:8). As my pastor likes to remind us, God is not surprised by the circumstances of our lives. He has a plan set in motion to provide us with all we could possibly need. Our part is to keep our eyes on Him and trust Him to do what only He can do!!

*12b  Work out (cultivate, carry out to the goal, and fully complete} your own salvation with reverence and awe and trembling (self-distrust, with serious caution, tenderness of conscience, watchfulness against temptation, timidly shrinking from whatever might offend God and discredit the name of Christ.)*
*13. [Not in your own strength] for it is God who is all the while effectually at work in you [energizing and creating in you the power and desire] both to will and to work for His good pleasure and satisfaction and delight.*
*Philippians 2:12b–13 (AMPC)*

Ready for our declaration?

**<u>"God, I believe that You are who You say You are and that You'll do what You say You'll do! I choose to put my complete trust in You. You are my hope and my salvation!</u>**

**<u>Today I say YES to You, Jesus!</u>**

# CHAPTER 7

# MARRIAGE AND MOTHERHOOD

I remember practicing some of what I have been taught when I approached marriage. As a young woman I had watched many of my friends get married, have children, and get divorced. I knew I wanted more than that. I was determined that I was going to do it right even if I had to wait longer than my friends had. I remember the day when a childhood friend came home on leave after joining the military straight out of high school. This guy was the class clown and a lot of fun, but I never thought of him like that. The fact is, I resented him a little bit. You see, my mom was our teacher at the private school, and I was the best student until this guy showed up. He seemingly never did homework and still got the best grades while always joking around and causing trouble. If you had told me back then that I would marry him, I would have laughed until I cried. But God had other plans.

Then there was the night he called me late, like 10:00 o'clock p.m., and wanted me to come over. He was on leave from the Navy and his parents lived just a few blocks from my house, so I consented even though it was late in the evening. He took me by total surprise when he kissed me on his front porch. I was not expecting that for sure. He told me he thought he loved me. Things progressed and eventually he asked me to marry him.

Eric was the kind of guy that decided on something and went for it. He decided it was time for him to get married and settle down with a good woman. He also decided that I was that good woman that he wanted to settle down with. Eric never does anything halfhearted or with a lot of forethought, so he just dived right in and kissed me and swept me off my feet so to speak. Not too long after this front porch experience, my mother came to talk to me and very soberly declared that Eric intended to propose to me. She wanted me to be prepared because he did not believe in the baptism of the Holy Spirit. Of course, she wanted the best for me and wanted me to be thinking about this. Since living a spirit-filled Christian life was important to me it was something I would want to share with the man I would spend the rest of my life with. Eric had told me before that he knew it was real because he couldn't deny that it was real for me, but it just wasn't for everybody. Well, as you might expect, when he proposed, I said yes. He will tell you that it was the beautiful big ring that got me. I will tell you that that's not exactly true, but either way the outcome was the same and I said yes. Then he went back out on the ship, and I went back to work pushing a broom. I became very afraid that I had made the wrong decision. I knew this was a big decision, and so, drawing from my upbringing, I did the only thing I knew to do and put a fleece before the Lord like Gideon did in Judges Chapter six. Eric was going to be gone for six months. Meanwhile, I worked at my janitorial job and prayed and cried and said, "Oh Lord, what have I done?" I was going to college as well and renting an apartment with my brother in the bigger city near where my mom lived. On Tuesdays, I had a two-hour break between classes, so I decided I would go to the park and fast my lunch hour and pray. I told the Lord that I just had to know that Eric was the right man for me if I were to marry him. So, I told the Lord that if he wanted me to marry Eric that I needed him to come home from that ship filled with the Holy Spirit. I was young and inexperienced at fasting, but I didn't know what else to do. I did this for about a month and as it turns out I got a letter in the mail from Eric telling me that he had been filled with the Holy Spirit. We have said that God is an individual God who works with us according to our natural inclinations. Eric was a hard sell because he's very intelligent and is good at reasoning things out. It must make sense, right? Here is His story, told in his words:

*I had just gotten engaged and was headed out to meet the USS Nimitz that was deployed on the Eastern Mediterranean. It had left without me, so it took time for me to get caught up with it. I flew from Norfolk, Virginia to Rota, Spain. While I was in Spain, I met another sailor who was full gospel, although I didn't know it at the time. He had the gift of speaking in tongues. Later I realized he was Spirit-filled. So, when we finally flew on board the ship, eventually I talked to him about it. I said, "Well, I am open to this Idea of being filled with the Spirit and speaking in tongues because my fiancé is. I might as well give it a try." I was kind of nervous. But he told me to meet him on the sponson at a certain time at night. A sponson is a little platform area outside the hull of the ship that is somewhat secluded. When I met him out there, he told me to lift my hands. Then he started speaking in tongues. As soon as he put hands on me, I immediately started speaking in tongues. I could not stop, even after we were done.*

*I remember the sponson was on the aft of the ship. The Nimitz is over three football fields long. I had to walk from the aft part of the ship to the front part of the ship where my berthing was. My berthing or rack is where I slept. I was on the 03 level of the ship, which is the highest level of the ship, underneath the flight deck. About every thirty feet or so there is what we call a knee knocker. This is where a watertight door could be attached. You have to step up and over a high threshold. So, I am walking along going past people. I was still speaking in tongues and couldn't stop. I remember thinking, "They must think I have lost my mind!" So, I made it all the way from aft to forward. I passed several people. They were just a blur in my vision. I made it all the way to my rack. I pulled the curtain and continued speaking in tongues for quite some time.*

Later I asked Eric what difference he noticed after this experience. After thinking about it, he told me he realized that he had more faith. He had a closer sense of who God is. Also, he said that when he was praying in tongues, he often was directed about how to pray in English about a particular matter.

Now Eric could not deny the veracity of the infilling of the Holy Spirit because he had just experienced it in a strong way. God was merciful to a young girl who just needed to know, and I am profoundly grateful for a mom who taught me the value of seeking the Lord and trusting Him to give me the answer I needed. That experience has walked me through over thirty-seven years of marriage. May I say right here that I am incredibly grateful for my husband's strength of character!! He did what I challenged you to do earlier in this book. He had the courage to give God a chance in an area he was convinced was not for him. He loved me and the Lord enough to open his heart to receive this gift, if it was something the Lord wanted him to have. Thank you, Lord, and thank you, Eric. And yes, I married the class clown, because God was gracious enough to assure me that it was part of his plan for me!

Another thing that really helped was a radio program by James Dobson. Doctor Dobson had a program that my mom always listened to when I was growing up. Doctor Dobson shared his story about how he and his wife made a commitment to each other when they got married to never consider divorce as an alternative to their problems. While Eric and I never had a written commitment, we made a verbal commitment to this, and we stuck with it. The truth is marriage is never easy because it involves two imperfect human beings who are trying to join their lives together into one happy family. We won't always agree. We won't always see things the same way, but we serve the same God, and we know what the standard of the Word says. So, we have survived, and we have grown closer to each other and closer to God. This is another one of those principles my mom taught me. If you can imagine for a moment a triangle with you and your spouse at the bottom two corners. The closer you each get to the Lord, who is at the top of the triangle, the closer you naturally get to each other as you go up to the point of the triangle. I have seen this happen in my marriage over time.

I mentioned that I learned to ride a motorcycle when I got married. What I did not relate was that I really had little choice. I learned the basics as a young girl. My uncle has a scary story about how he taught me. He took me to the school parking lot where we had plenty of room. When we arrived, he got off and had me scoot up to the driving position. I don't recall his exact instructions, but I distinctly remember his expression when I turned the throttle too hard, and the bike did a wheely, and I landed on the ground. ☺ Thankfully both the bike and I survived. My uncle, on the other hand, had a fright that took some time to get over. Ha!

So, my new husband and I loaded up my station wagon with my few belongings tucked around my prized possession, my grandmother's vanity and stool. We were heading to Jacksonville, Florida where He was stationed in the Navy.

We were making good time, enjoying being together on an adventure. All was good until it wasn't, as they say. We were in rush hour traffic in Atlanta, Georgia when the car began to overheat. There we were in one of the two center lanes of a four-lane interstate and the car just quit. Ironically, I don't remember the details of how we got there but we ended up at a repair shop that helped us, after hours of waiting, to get back on the road. It was very traumatic for a young, naïve, newly married girl, but I survived.

When we arrived in Florida, we felt relieved as we pulled into the driveway of Eric's trailer. As it turned out, the car had a cracked block and suddenly our only form of transportation was his 450 Kawasaki motorcycle. After a quick refresher course, I was forced to get comfortable with driving that thing. I can remember trips to the grocery store with me on the back holding a paper bag of groceries on each side and Eric with one between his legs while he navigated us toward home, which thankfully was close by.

Marriage was a new beginning for me. I had moved away from everything I knew. So, there was a lot for me to learn. I would have to find a new church. I would have to develop new friendships, get a job somewhere, etc. It was a scary, exciting time for me!!

The first year of our marriage Eric was gone for 10 of those 12 months. I spent a lot of time alone. I went to work. I went to Church and then went home to play with my pet ferret and relax until it was time to wake in the morning and hit repeat.

One night, as I was returning home from church, I turned the corner towards our trailor and was confronted by firetrucks. I remember thinking, "Oh, dear, someone has had a fire." Then the realization struck me that I was that someone. My home was on fire. We lost almost everything, including my pet ferret. sadly, I lost my prized vanity. One of the few things that we were able to salvage was a photo album containing our wedding pictures. It had been in a box in the back of the closet. It was a little brown around the edges, but I was determined to keep it! Thank God for my church family! They took up an offering. People donated items I would need to start over again. Our landlord provided us with a different trailor, and I was able to get things set up before Eric returned home. Talk about a lesson in trusting God! He certainly took care of me throughout that experience, and I am grateful for the people he placed around me! I realize those people are a direct response to my praying mom in Iowa! (Don't give up Moms!)

So, we had our first child after having been married for over a year. Fact is, we really didn't try until after the first year. Like I said, Eric had gone out to sea that first year. Then it took another year of trying.

I was beginning to be convinced that I would never realize my dream of being a mother. But God, being the faithful God that He is, did indeed bring me a beautiful little boy when I was twenty-five. I always smile about this because I remember my grandmother telling me that I couldn't get married until I was at least twenty-five. I remember thinking, when my first child came along, "Well, Grandma, at least I waited until I was twenty-five to have my first child!" 😊 As you can well imagine, I was absorbed in my newfound status as mother. My world revolved around that precious little boy with his beautiful soft blonde curls and big beautiful dark eyes. He was so precious. everybody thought he was a girl, even when I dressed him in bib overhauls and a flannel shirt, they just didn't get it. Of course, it didn't help that I couldn't bring myself to cut those soft, curly locks. I remember my husband sitting me down and reminding me that when our children were grown and gone that we would still need a good foundation in our marriage to build on. He implored me to put priority on our relationship and not let my newfound status as a mother get in between our relationship. While that made me mad initially, I knew he was right, so we went on regular dates with me always worried about babysitters that I didn't trust. I remember a particular time when I agreed to let one of Eric's coworkers watch the kids. (We had three by this time.) I came home to my youngest with black permanent marker drawn around his eyes. He looked like a raccoon. I found the babysitter on the couch, and I went upstairs and found a black permanent marker on the walls upstairs. I was upset and didn't want to pay this chick, but Eric insisted, and I had to let it go, because I knew he was right. However, she was never watching my kids again. That's all I had to say! The thing is, the black marker eventually faded, and my children survived without any real damage. Our relationship, meanwhile, continued though shaky for a few days.

I remember being very anxious and worried about everything that had to do with my son. I was worried about how this was going to affect him, or how that was going to cause him problems in the future. I remember reading statistics about how three-fourths of a child's personality is formed by the time they're five years old. I was working full time and desperately wishing I could stay home and just be with my baby, but God had me in the workforce for a reason that I understand now but didn't then.

There was a particular Wednesday night that God chose to teach me a valuable lesson. I was in the nursery again because there was no one there to watch the children. The church that we were attending had a fellowship hall behind the sanctuary which is where the nursery was also located. One night I was standing in the nursery window close to tears when the youth pastor came through the door that connected the sanctuary and the fellowship hall. He said, "Hello," and proceeded to the kitchen to get himself a cup of coffee. He got all the way back to the door leading to the sanctuary when he stopped, turned around and said these words to me, "Miss Brenda, Patrick's going to be okay." It hit me like a ton of bricks, and, of course, I cried. The fact is it still brings tears to my eyes. To think that God loved me so much that he stopped that young man and had him encourage me and remind me that ultimately my children and their future were in His hands only. That day I took another step closer to trusting Him completely.

Then there was the time I was expecting our second child. I had had a particularly long day and a sleepless night because I was very pregnant, and my daughter wanted to push off my belly button from the inside. When Eric came home from work and was preparing to go play soccer, he saw that I was struggling. So, he suggested that he take Patrick, who was just shy of three years old at the time, with him to the soccer field to give me a break. My response was an immediate and definite, "No, that's fine. He needs to stay here. He needs to get to bed at a good time." What was really going through my mind, however, was that I knew Eric would not watch him carefully. My husband is normally very attentive to me and his kids except when he's playing soccer. Soccer is one of his biggest passions, and at the time, when he saw a soccer ball that would be his complete focus. I just knew he wouldn't be watching Patrick carefully, and so many things could go wrong, and I was fearful. As it turns out, I had been asked to speak at the next women's ministry meeting at our church. The next day when I was studying for that meeting, I had my outline all done and all ready. I was feeling fairly good about the message and was ready to deliver it later that evening. As I was praying, the Lord began to deal with me about my attitude the night before. He reminded me once again that my children were ultimately in his hands not my husband's. His reprimand went something like this: "*If you do not trust your husband with your children ultimately you are not trusting me.*" Can I say, "Ouch!!"? That one was hard to swallow. It was even harder to swallow when the Lord proceeded to tell me to share this message with the women that I was about to speak with that evening. So instead of giving them a feel-good kind of message, I had to give them the same admonition that God had given me. Apparently, someone besides me needed to hear that. And it is a good lesson to learn. We can trust other people (like babysitters or even doctors) if we understand and know that ultimately God is the one who's in control. Remember, people will fail us, but God never will. Another step taken towards trusting God completely was taken that day.

*Some trust in chariots and some in horses, but we will remember and trust in the name of the Lord our God.*
***Psalms 20:7 (AMP)***

It seems that God had a lesson for me to learn with each child, so, fast forward. Eric is out to sea again, and I had gone back to Iowa to stay with my mother while he was gone for six months. Our daughter was about seven months old or so when the Lord began to talk to me about having another child. This was not part of my perfect plan. I had my little boy and my little girl. I had stepped into being the mom I always wanted to be. I was good.

Well, I kept having the same thing come into my mind while I was in prayer. The Lord wanted us to have another child. Finally, I conceded and told the Lord, "Okay, but you are going to have to tell Eric! I am not saying a word." Once again, I am so glad that God is patient with us. As it turned out, in our correspondence, Eric expressed his feeling that God wanted us to have another child 😊. So, I had the confirmation that I needed, and three weeks after Eric came home from Sea Duty, I was pregnant with our youngest son.

As I mentioned earlier, my husband was in the Navy, so, we moved around a lot. One thing I learned early was to trust God every time we were up for transfer to a new duty station. Somewhere along the line we adopted the following scripture as our motto:

*The steps of a [good] man are directed and established by the Lord when He delights in his way [and He busies himself with his every step]. Though he falls, he shall not be utterly cast down, for the Lord grasps his hand in support and upholds him.*
*(Psalms 37:23,24 AMPC)*

Just imagine God Almighty who "busies himself" to prepare a place for my foot to fall each time I take a step!

We came to understand that while the Navy dictated our choice of duty stations, ultimately, God was in control if we would simply trust Him.

Our first duty station was in Jacksonville, Florida. We were both working full-time jobs. He worked the late-night shift, and I was usually working second shift. I worked for a small security company that after being bought out more than once jumped from small time to the big leagues. During this time, I went from being a security officer just trying to stay awake during a twelve-hour shift where I barely saw a single person to being the Regional Coordinator for the head boss. Remember I said that I longed to be a stay-at-home mom, but God had other plans. Also, God knows our future and will prepare us for that future if we will "cooperate with the program" as my mother would say.

The first promotion I got was to sergeant. The contractor's head guy used to call me "sergeant of the guards." After some time, I was asked to consider taking a position in the office as their personnel manager.

Well, I was scared, but willing, so I talked to Eric, and we agreed the thing to do was go with it and see what happened. It meant more money, which we, of course, could use. My job was to trust God to help me with this new position. As I mentioned, It wasn't long before this small company was bought out by a large corporation, and I got my first taste of big corporate power. I went from hiring for a handful of posts to overseeing personnel for a company more than double our size and not only permanent posts but temporary posts where we might need a person for only three weeks. I found my naive self in charge of hiring, training, outfitting, fingerprinting, and arming both permanent and temporary employees for a very large company. To say that I grew as a person is putting it lightly. God was gracious to me, and I survived. My first shock came on my first day with the new company, when, expecting to be trained alongside their current personnel manager, I instead found myself on my own. That afternoon, they called their current personnel manager into the office and let her go, and suddenly, I was left to fend for myself.

As I have said, God was faithful to me. I did the best I could, but it wasn't easy. My new boss was a workaholic who expected everyone else to work long hours just like him. I hung in there and it wasn't too long before I fell into routine. I did the best I could, and the Lord helped me to do a decent job. I became adept at knowing what size uniform a person wore just by looking at them. I didn't mind all the paperwork or the training part. It was just the ability to read people (or my lack thereof) that stressed me out. By this time, I was pregnant with our first child, and my stress level was high. I found myself constantly in fear of making the wrong choice, hiring the wrong person, etc. Then came along a new district manager that is still the best boss I have ever had. He was kind and considerate. I remember him coming into my office after 5 pm and asking, "why are you still here?" When I explained that our former boss would never have thought of releasing us earlier, I was promptly informed that from then on 5 p.m. was quitting time, no matter what. What a blessing!! Somewhere along the line, my new boss, concerned about the stress of my job affecting my pregnancy, presented me with a proposition. He asked if I would be willing to take over the receptionist job, at least until after I had the baby. Then, if I wanted to return to personnel, I could do so. I couldn't have been happier to be away from personnel!! It's a long story but as I continued to do the best I could doing the work presented to me, God kept promoting me.

Patrick was born and after five weeks of maternity leave, I returned to work. I don't remember my boss ever asking if I wanted to return to Personnel and I sure wasn't going to mention it. I was happy continuing in my current position as a receptionist, and it seemed my boss was happy as well.

Time went by and circumstances changed. Eventually I was asked to become the boss's Administrative Assistant when his current assistant got married and was planning to move away. I remember telling my boss that I had flunked typing in High School and asked if he was he sure wanted me. I would be typing proposals, etc. He said he had been watching me and was confident that I could do the job. So, I agreed, and I was sent for some training. I worked hard and the Lord helped me to succeed.

I would like to take a side bar and share something. I don't remember where in the progression of promotions that I received while employed with this security company it happened, but I had a breakdown. I remember coming home to tell Eric that I had been offered another promotion. I was crying and saying that I wasn't sure if

I wanted to take it or not. All I ever wanted was to be a stay-at-home mom, after all. Looking back, I thank God for my wonderful level-headed husband who helped me realize that these promotions were not by accident and surely it was God Himself that was behind it. Shouldn't we trust Him regardless of how bad I wanted to be at home?

So, I stepped into the new job with as much zeal as I knew how to give. I helped with payroll. I helped put together a database for our employees and generally made myself useful.

Time passed, and eventually, my boss was promoted from District Manager to Regional Vice President. The day when he called me into his office and told me about his promotion, his next words really blew me away. He said, "I told them I would take the promotion on one condition, and that was that they would promote you with me." Wow! Talk about God's favor!! Now I would be in a separate office where I would handle all the paperwork for the Region. I was often there alone as my boss traveled a lot among the different offices in the region. This suited my independent nature and spoke to how much my boss trusted me. He would often tell me that if I was tired (by this time, I was very pregnant with our second child) that he wanted me to turn the phones over to the district office and make use of the couch in his office to rest. I could never bring myself to do that, but what a blessing, right!?!?!? Suddenly, I was making more money than my husband including quarterly bonuses. I was free from all the stress I had been under before. I was learning that God rewarded faithful obedience.

One last story about my journey as a mother and I will move on, I promise.

When we were stationed in Norfolk, Virginia, Patrick was preschool age. True to form, I worried about every detail. This time it was about school. Should we send him to public school, or should we homeschool? I honestly didn't feel like I was up to the task but there was a lot of pressure from well-meaning Christians in my circle who insisted homeschooling was the only answer in today's society. I couldn't argue with that, and yet I felt hesitant. I got busy and did my best to teach Patrick his colors and even his ABC's. I was doing my best to prepare him for a free preschool program the Navy had if our child qualified.

The day came when I anxiously took Patrick for testing. I was shocked when they came to me and said that there was nothing for them to teach him. Patrick already knew everything in their curriculum. I went home still facing the problem of whether to send him to public school or try homeschooling him. To most, this would seem like a sign that homeschooling was indeed the answer, but I still did not have peace of mind regarding this issue. So, we prayed and asked God to show us what to do.

I honestly don't remember the circumstances surrounding how God answered, except that He led me to a particular scripture:

*I do not ask that You will take them out of the world, but that You will keep and protect them from the evil one.*
*(John 17:15 AMPC)*

This was a prayer that Jesus prayed over his disciples and for us as well. I took this to mean that the Lord wanted us to go ahead and send our kids to public school. They would need to be 'in' the world but not 'of' the world. So, when they started school, I would pray this scripture over them and send them on their way, knowing that my Heavenly Father would watch over them! Let me make it clear that this was God's answer for our children. I have nothing against homeschooling, in fact, my best friend has done a fantastic job homeschooling her children and even helps with her grandchildren. Homeschooling was the answer for her family. If this is an issue for you then I encourage you to find God's answer for you and your family!

## Important Principle

All my life I had been taught the principle of tithing. While I would like to say that I have always been faithful in this area, I will say that as I grew older, I came to understand the value of giving faithfully to the Lord. You may have heard that this is the only command with a promise and a challenge to test the Lord. (Check out Malachai 3:10, 11). So, I came into my marriage with this principle firmly in place in my life. Eric, however, had not been taught the same as I had been. It took me some time to establish employment. Since I handled the bills, I did not tithe on Eric's income out of respect for him, because he did not have the same convictions as I did on the subject. When I did start working and time passed, and Eric saw how God was blessing and promoting me on my job. God began to work on his heart regarding this matter. You see, when I started working, I asked Eric's permission to tithe on my paycheck, and he agreed. I was thrilled the day Eric leaned over during church one Sunday morning service and simply stated that he would like me to start tithing on his paycheck as well. We have never looked back. I would like to say that we lived in abundance from then on, but that isn't exactly true. However, I can say that as we were faithful to follow God's plan, we never went without. God always supplied all our needs. We understood that we had a responsibility to steward our finances well no matter how much or how little we had, and God was faithful to take care of our needs.

*Give, and it will be given to you. They will pour into your lap a good measure — pressed down, shaken together, and running over [with no space left for more]. For with the standard of measurement you use [when you do good to others], it will be measured to you in return. (Luke 6:38 AMPC)*

Ready for our declaration?

**<u>"God, I believe that You are who You say You are and that You'll do what You say You'll do! I choose to put my complete trust in You. You are my hope and my salvation!</u>**

**<u>Today I say YES to You, Jesus!</u>**

65

## CHAPTER 8
# DESIRES FULFILLED.

While I enjoyed my new position with the new security company, I still hungered to be able to stay at home with my children. I remember enduring comments from a certain well-meaning grandma type from church. She would say something like, "Honey, don't you realize how much your children need you to be at home?" She couldn't know how much I ached to be able to do just that. And yet, I knew I was where God wanted me to be. Tempted though I was to give in to her pressure, as well as my own selfish desire, I kept moving forward in obedience the best way I knew how.

Then the day finally came when we were up for orders. Eric and I had talked and decided that the time had come for me to stay home after our transfer. There was a lot to consider!! We had bought a house, so we would need to find renters. And ironically, then I had to deal with a different kind of pressure.

When we got our orders, we were going to be heading from Jacksonville, Florida to Norfolk, Virginia. The District office for the same security company I was working for just happened to need an administrative assistant in their office in Norfolk, and, of course, my boss had recommended me for the job. They practically begged me to come work for them. So, the temptation was there. We were making good money after all. However, God was offering me the desire of my heart and I had my husband's blessing, so I was happy to turn down the offer and become truly a stay-at-home mom for the first time. God was gracious in helping us find renters in a timely manner which helped in the decision-making process also. I was eight months pregnant with my daughter when we moved to Norfolk, Virginia. Keep in mind that during all this, Eric was out to sea a large portion of the time, so I had the responsibility of the children and the household as well as keeping a steady flow of letters sent to him while he was gone.

## PASSION DEVELOPED

It all started one Sunday morning, during Sunday School. Folks were chatting when the discussion about wives in the kitchen came up. Eric made a jokingly derogatory comment about me and my lack of abilities in the kitchen. Granted, we had been subsisting on hamburger helper and macaroni and cheese. His comment, while not intended to be hurtful, caused something to rise within me. It was like a challenge! I had to prove him wrong! It was then that the Lord began to develop in me a new love. I had always liked to bake. As a young girl I learned to make cookies and was pretty good at it. Remember, my mother was a single mother from the time I was eleven, so she seldom had time to teach me much in the kitchen. I do remember watching her, and I guess I must have learned a lot from her by just watching. She was so busy trying to hold things together that she seldom had time to slow down and teach me how to do what she did best. Later, as a young wife and mother, I can remember calling Mom and asking her how she made this or that. I still have handwritten instructions that she gave me on how to make some of my favorites. I also remember being frustrated with her "put a little of this and a little of that" type of instructions in there. I had to ask her to be a little more specific ☺. As time passed, I developed a true passion for baking. I truly loved being in the kitchen. As I have said, my mother is my hero, and I wanted to grow up and be just like her. It never ceases to amaze me how Mom could feed folks with such ease. Whenever we came home for a visit, she would begin pulling things out of the 'fridge and before we knew it, we had a feast set before us seemly without effort. She knew how to plan ahead.

So, I was determined to get better in the kitchen, and I did. While I excelled at baked goods, I did well in other areas also. Cooking magazines like Taste of Home became my favorite reading material. I could get lost in one of those if I weren't careful. To this day, nothing gives me more pleasure than to see folks enjoy the food I make. I have often prayed and asked the Lord to guard my heart against pride. I never want it to be about me. I have even questioned the validity of this passion. Is it just a selfish thing, or is it something that God has given me that He intends for me to use for his glory? I have concluded that this passion is indeed a God-given desire, and it is my job to steward it well. I believe that Psalms 37:4, where it talks about God giving us the desires of our hearts, has a double meaning. Namely, God puts desires in our hearts and then proceeds to fulfill them as we walk in obedience to him. I know it doesn't make a lot of sense. I have struggled with this idea myself. I remember being at the altar feeling foolish as I tearfully told my pastor that I had this passion, and I didn't know what to do with it. There are times when I still don't know what to do with it, but I try my best to honor the Lord with it as often as I can. My whole point is, if you have a passion that consumes you, consider that it is very possible that God has put that in you for a purpose. My advice to you is to strive to always honor the Lord while pursuing your passion. You may find yourself unable to function in what I call your area of anointing right now, but your time will come when God is ready for you to do so.

Okay, so I enjoyed eleven years as a stay-at-home mom. It was a bit of a sacrifice for sure!! Our budget was tight, but we made it through while continuing to be faithful with our tithes. I developed my talents in the kitchen, partly out of necessity. I had to learn how to stretch the dollar to be able to feed a family of five. It was a time of challenge and blessing.

By this time, we were transferred to Meridian, Mississippi. The church there was experiencing revival or so it seemed to me. Our pastor at the time had been to the Brownsville Revival and his passion was truly contagious! I was so excited about what God was doing. The pastor was one of those amazing people who are so on fire for the Lord that they shine God's holy light on you and sometimes make you slightly uncomfortable while at the same time you are drawn to them. He loved God and was challenging us to draw closer to God as well, no matter what the cost. I was so excited to see God moving. I was young and naive and didn't realize that trouble was brewing. Eric and I were leading the Children's church and were in the Choir. I do remember hearing whispers about things changing when January came along. The night came when Eric was on temporary duty away from home and I was attending the church business meeting. To my horror, they voted the pastor out that night. I was devastated, to say the least. I had never heard of such a thing, to start with, and couldn't believe God's people capable of doing something to someone who was simply going after God with all his heart and shepherding his people accordingly. The truth was these people were uncomfortable with the changes God was asking them to make so they went after the pastor. I called Eric when I got home and told him what had happened. He was as upset as I was but wisely advised me not to do anything until he got home. So, until we got clear direction from the Lord, we stayed put. We loved on the pastor and his family. We helped them pack up their belongings and even witnessed the day they pulled out of the parking lot after shaking the dust off their feet. That body of believers had missed God. Finally, God gave my husband release, and we were freed to find a new church home. This was the one and only time that I had ever left a church for reasons other than a marriage and military transfer.

We found ourselves at our current church, First

Assembly of God, and we are blessed to be a part of a body of believers and leadership that goes after God and follows His lead in all things. We took time to heal from the breakup of our previous church. I spent a lot of time at the altar, and God was gracious to give us that time. It wasn't too long before the Lord began to nudge me to get involved in the life of the church. Grieving time was over, and it was time to get busy. I started out by joining the choir and was soon asked to be a part of the ensemble. I loved it! We sang cantatas and my voice was stretched from an average soprano to someone who could hit the high notes.

I remember living on the Navy base and baking a bunch of goodies to bring every Sunday to share in the kitchen. Again, I loved doing it, even though it meant getting up early. I loved the church and dreaded the day we would have to leave.

When it was time for new orders, it seems it was time to test my resolve to trust God. Eric called one memorable day to inform me that he had just accepted orders to Naples, Italy. Have you ever seen a cartoon where someone slams their back against the wall and slides down in despair?? That was me. I knew very little about Italy, but I was pretty sure that the mafia was in there somewhere and he was telling me we were taking our three children to a mafia infested country. Are you kidding me right now?!?!? Eric patiently explained to me that it was highly unusual for the military to allow a family with small children to transfer overseas. Surely, the Lord was in this move just like He had been in all our previous transfers.

It took me some time to pray through that one, for

sure, but pray I did, and I finally got it in my head that God had indeed directed this step in our journey just like He had every transfer we had taken so far. I am so glad that I did. I started getting excited and looked for ways to prepare myself. I went to the library and got teaching tapes on the language and tried to learn all that I could.

Our experience in Italy was life-changing, to say the least. We met an Italian family that we still call family to this day. We embraced the culture and enjoyed it immensely! Our Italian family loved Eric especially. My husband has never met a stranger, and they loved his pantomime ways of communicating!! We met them when we first moved out of temporary housing. This was away from any military facility as we chose not to live in military housing. They stayed in a two-bedroom apartment a few doors down from us. We found out that this was their summer home. Many Italians take the month of August off as their vacation. They usually have a place where the whole family (there were nineteen in our friend's family staying there at the time) comes together to hang out. It was during this time that we met them. My goofy husband, who spoke virtually no Italian was up in their 'fridge looking for something good to eat. They loved him for it. I learned very quickly to come out of my shell. These demonstrative people wouldn't let me stay in my happy place. It was during this experience that I have come to believe that every American should experience a different culture! What we call common sense is often just something that is familiar to our culture. People of other cultures do not think the same as we do. I learned that family is very important to them. Senior parents aren't sent to a nursing home but rather taken into their children's homes to be cared for. Children are pampered up to a certain age. Crime against children was almost unheard of there. It took me three weeks to try driving there. It seems that you were only supposed to stop at certain stop signs, otherwise you would experience all sorts of hand gestures that were not very nice. I was introduced to the roundabout and so many one-way streets that it was intimidating to say the least. Oh, and if an Italian tells you he will do something "*dopodomani*" (the day after tomorrow) be advised that he really means never, lol!

While in Italy, I went back to college since all the kids were now of school age. I learned the language and became semi-fluent. The problem was that most of our Italian friends spoke a dialect instead of proper Italian. I remember Babbo (Dad) teasing me and asking me why I didn't speak better Italian. I responded with the same question☺. He just grinned with that twinkle he always had in his eye. I sure do miss that guy!!

The overall experience left us with a deep-seated love for Italy and a question as to why God had led us there. Perhaps someday I will meet an Italian here in the US who needs an interpreter?? Meanwhile, we stay in contact with our Italian "family" and have gone back to visit a couple of times and look forward to doing so again soon.

While there, we started going to a church that had the name of Assembly of God attached to it. However, it wasn't really overseen by the Assembly. During that time, I know that God was stretching both of us. Do you remember what I said at the beginning, that if we would keep saying "yes" to God and allow Him to, He would stretch our capacity to fit His purposes for our lives? This was one of those times. It wasn't until later that I realized just how much God had done in both of us.

We did as we always do and tried to plug into the church the best we could. Here we experienced another culture. Most of the church consisted of folks from Africa, both Nigeria and Ghana. They are wonderful people, and so exuberant in worship. Most were in Italy earning money to send home to their families. Many left their children in Africa because they felt they could get a better education there. What a sacrifice this must have been for them! These people knew about supernatural powers. They understood and didn't have any problem believing in God's supernatural power. The problem was, because they had seen it firsthand in their home country, they were still afraid of the supernatural power of the enemy. They would come and get saved again and again, not realizing that the power of God that lived in them as Christians was stronger and more powerful than that of the enemy.

It was here during this season of our lives that we became involved in leading worship. It wasn't really a big deal. It consisted of singing with CD's.

It was also during this time that God began to do a work in my husband that was not evident until later. We had become good friends with a gal who worked with the kids and found out that she had a moment of weakness and allowed the (married) pastor to kiss her. Obviously, we had a problem. There was no oversight of the church, but this needed to be dealt with. Our friend was certainly repentant, and the pastor had taken advantage of her vulnerability. This needed to be dealt with and you guessed it, we were it. Eric talked with a couple of other leaders. and Eric was elected to confront the Pastor. The pastor acted like it was no big deal and wasn't repentant at all. He was asked to leave, and we were faced with a body of believers who needed guidance through this season. The Lord used me, Eric, and another leader to continue with the ministry of that church until we left. It was tough, but we did our best and the Lord helped us.

*Trust (lean on, rely on, and be confident) in the Lord and do good; so shall you dwell in the land and feed faithfully, and truly you shall be fed.*

*Delight yourself also in the Lord, and He will give you the desires and secret petitions of your heart.*
*Psalms 37:3,4 (AMPC)*

Ready for our declaration?

**"God, I believe that You are who You say You are and that You'll do what You say You'll do! I choose to put my complete trust in You. You are my hope and my salvation!**

**Today I say YES to You, Jesus!**

## CHAPTER 9

# THE NEXT SEASON

So fast forward to the next transfer. It was not by accident that orders for Meridian, MS were offered to us. Both of us had no question but that God was leading us back to Meridian. Truth be told, First Assembly Meridian was the hardest church to leave in all our military career. We felt like we were coming home.

Ironically, when we arrived back in Mississippi, we discovered that the church was without a worship pastor. I was horrified when Eric said, "I know who they need as worship leader, you!" I couldn't believe my ears!! Me?? What was he thinking? Eric has always had more confidence in me than I could ever have in myself. Fact is, I call him my self-confidence. There is something in me that wants to make him proud, so when he puts a challenge in front of me, I am ready to give it a try. This, however, was asking too much. You guessed it, our pastor came to me and asked if I would be willing to lead the church in worship at least temporarily until they could find a full-time worship pastor. God is merciful and gave me some help. I led the singing while someone more musical than myself had oversight for picking out the song lists and directing the musicians. That "temporary" arrangement lasted 5 years. During this time, God was stretching my capacity to fit His purpose for me. I learned to depend on Him. I experienced what I call "God Confidence" where something other than myself would rise within me and I was able to truly lead people to worship the Lord. I learned a lot, not the least of which was how to lead people God's way. I have always been a follower and had no natural inclination to lead. God needed to develop this quality in me. It was hard to learn, but necessary for me, I know.

I need to note here that when we returned to Mississippi, I became aware of a change in my husband that I hadn't realized was taking place. Before Italy, Eric was not truly engaged with church. Don't get me wrong, he came and was serving the Lord. However, his passion (soccer) often caused him to miss services. I remember feeling sorry for myself as I looked at the empty seat beside me wishing he were there with me instead of at some soccer tournament. I felt like I had experienced enough time with him out to sea and me sitting in church alone that I shouldn't have to endure his absence because of soccer. And yet, there we were. It wasn't until we returned from Italy that it appeared that God had done a work in Eric's heart. He was suddenly more engaged, and I watched God use him to tell one of our friends to "get over it" as she expressed her anger at God for allowing her mother to die (which was her excuse for not being in church). Only someone like Eric would get away with that, for sure!! Since then, my husband has been very invested in fellowship with believers in our church.

Where before he never really had friends in the church, now he enjoys friendships with godly men in our church, not the least of which is our pastor and associate pastor. I am so grateful for a man who has allowed God to stretch his capacity to fit God's purpose for His life. The fact is, we have a couple that have become our best friends. They are family in the truest sense. Eric has been a deacon and is now the Church Executive Treasurer. He is invested in reaching others for God using his God-given ability to interact with people with such ease. Thank You Lord for a godly husband!!

Here I would like to say that when we returned to Mississippi, I had had the privilege to be a stay-at-home mom for almost eleven years. It was sometime after we returned that I had a strong test in my ability to trust God no matter what. I mean, it's easy to do that when things are going your way, right?!? I think I mentioned that when we were at our first duty station in Jacksonville, Florida, we bought a house. So, when we got transferred, we had to rent it out. This arrangement went well until it didn't. We lost our renters. Now I had no choice but to go back to work. I was devastated, but it was inevitable that I would need to do so to help cover an extra house payment. Looking back, I realize that trusting God is something we must do, even, maybe especially, when we don't like our current circumstances and when we don't know what the future holds! I would like to say I handled this with grace, but I would be lying, for sure. Anyway, God was very good to me and supplied me with a job in the school system, which meant I would be able to be home when the kids were home. Thank you, Lord, for that!!

I don't know all of God's reasons for allowing this season in my life, but I do know that I grew as a person and it didn't kill me after all, 😊. Perhaps I was there for more than one reason. Perhaps the Lord was able to use me to encourage and bless someone else. It's ironic how self-focused we can be!

So, I spent nearly three years working in the school system. My youngest son was at the same elementary school with me which was good for both of us. I assisted in a kindergarten class the first year and did tutoring and assisted in a first-grade class the following two years.

## RETIREMENT

The day of retirement came after many years of dreaming about it. Over the years leading up to this, we spent time talking to the Lord about our dreams for the future. We had it all figured out, of course. We realized we wanted to stay in Mississippi. We wanted a house out in the country with a lake. We wanted the privacy the country could afford. A place where the kids had freedom to enjoy the outdoors. Where we could have outside pets with no worries.

When the time came, we had decisions to make. We would be moving school districts, which affected our kids, especially Patrick who was a Sophomore in High School with lots of friends he didn't want to leave. Would I possibly be able to stay at home now?

This was one of the rare times when I had more faith than Eric. I think I mentioned before that Eric has the gift of Faith and is a total optimist! Eric was feeling the pressure of taking care of his family for the first time in many years. Before, it was the military steering the ship, so to speak. Now, he felt the burden was his alone. I, on the other hand, just knew God had a plan.

Mom was visiting and we were enjoying house hunting adventures while poor Eric was sweating the details. When she and I stepped into the front door of our current home I just knew! It is hard to explain but I felt a blanket of warmth that said, "this is home" settle on me. The trouble is it wasn't in the country with a lake. In fact, it was in the city limits a mile away from the church. Once Eric was able to see for himself, he agreed with us that this was the place.

Our home sits in a quiet neighborhood where we were one of only two houses on our side of the street until just recently. Traffic is minimal. The house itself is two stories with lots of room and the kitchen was a dream for me as a baker. We were home.

God took care of Eric's worries by providing him with a job on the military base. The kids survived the school transfer making new friends. The advantage of being so close to the church has been a blessing also.

We moved in, vowing to do our best to use our house to honor the Lord. We have had many gatherings in our home, taking advantage of the space we have and the close proximity to the church which makes it easy for folks to find us.

We did decide that I could stay home and be a homemaker again. It was a blessing to be able to volunteer at the church and be a part of the ministry there. I had the privilege of painting the new sanctuary, sewing costumes for a yearly program we put on at Christmas, etc. I enjoyed it for sure.

After three years, Eric took a job working for a fast food establishment. We became the family that all worked for this company, including all three of our children. Once the kids were older, I found myself going back to work again. I managed a different branch of the store for a while, and later took a job sitting with an elderly couple. That ended when the folk's sons decided to have only CNAs caring for their parents. They even offered to pay for me to get the training so I could stay on, but I didn't feel like that was the direction the Lord wanted me to go, so I decided not to continue with them.

From this point on, I spent most of my time working at my husband's store. Even when I wasn't working full-time hours for him, someone would call out and I would get an SOS call from my husband, and off to the rescue I would go.

*5) Lean on, trust in, and be confident in the Lord with all your heart and mind and do not rely on your own insight or understanding. 6)In all your ways know, recognize, and acknowledge Him, and He will direct and make straight and plain your paths. Proverbs 3:5,6 (AMPC)*

Ready for our declaration?

**<u>"God, I believe that You are who You say You are and that You'll do what You say You'll do! I choose to put my complete trust in You. You are my hope and my salvation!</u>**

**<u>Today I say YES to You, Jesus!</u>**

## CHAPTER 10

# ACCELERATED TRAINING:

One day, back when I was sitting with the folks, my single daughter, who was in her second year of college, called to tell me that she was pregnant. Wow, that hit me so hard. This was my good little girl. The one of all my children that never really gave me any trouble during her school years. The devil was quick to accuse! He told me I was a terrible mother!! I didn't pray hard enough; I didn't give wise enough council. It was all my fault. You name it, the devil made sure to throw every accusation he could at me. This came during the last half hour of my shift. By the time I was on the way home, the Lord comforted me with the scripture that "All things work together for good to those who love God and are called according to his purpose." (Romans 8:28) The Amplified says it like this:

*We are assured and know that [God being a partner in their labor] all things work together and are [fitting into a plan] for good to and for those who love God and are called according to [His] purpose.*
*(Romans 8:28 AMPC)*

I love this scripture because it helps me realize that even when we mess things up, our faithful God is still there ready to work things out for our good. All we must do is keep our eyes on him. Then dust ourselves off, ask forgiveness, and forge ahead with the Lord!!

I remember hiding on the balcony of our church during the Youth Convention. This was usually one of my favorite times at church. There is nothing like a sanctuary full of young kids worshipping with all their hearts. The atmosphere would always be electric! Usually, I enjoy this so much. However, if I hadn't previously committed myself, honestly, I would have been hiding at home instead. As it was, I had, indeed, volunteered and knew It wasn't right to back out, so, after receiving my initial instructions, I headed for the darkest corner of the balcony I could find. I didn't want to talk about it, and I knew that if a certain well-meaning friend got a notion that something was up, she would be right there pulling it out of me. I was in no mood to be kind. The thought, though weakly spoken in my mind, was, "God, you've got this, right?" It felt more like a squeak than a true thought, but it was at that moment that I experienced the closest thing to the audible voice of the Lord that I had ever heard. Just as plain as day I heard the Lord say to me, "If you believe that, then say so, out loud, every time you have a doubt or fear about this issue. Say '**Lord, I trust you with my daughter's future!**'" As I meditated on this mandate from the Lord, He helped me to realize three important things about using my voice to speak such a declaration. (Remember – there is power of life and death in the tongue – Proverbs 18:21)

1. The Lord hears me, and it becomes a form of worship to Him.
2. I hear it, and it serves to re-affirm to myself that I do indeed trust in God. This always reminds me of how David encouraged himself in the Lord. He was always giving himself a pep talk.
3. The enemy of my soul hears it, and it becomes a declaration. Like a line in the sand that he isn't allowed to cross, because I am a child of the king and so I'm off limits to him!

*Death and life are in the power of the tongue, and they who indulge in it shall eat the fruit of it [for death or life]*
*Proverbs 18:21 AMPC*

*For by your words, you will be justified and acquitted, and by your words you will be condemned and sentenced.*
*Matthew 12:37*
*(AMPC)*

This became a pivotal point in my ability to trust God. I realized that I had no recourse but to trust God, after all. I was powerless to change the circumstances anyway, so why was I wasting my time worrying about the uncertain future?

I would love to say that everything was peaches and cream and smooth sailing. However, it was not. There were many moments of anxiety and times when I didn't act at all like I trusted the Lord. I struggled with the "what if's" and the uncertainty of my daughter's future. However, taking one day at a time, I made it through this season and found that God really was faithful. There was never a day that He wasn't there taking care of me and my daughter. Two beautiful things came out of this situation – you guessed it, my first grandchild, a boy, was born and later my granddaughter. Becoming a grandmother, "Nanny" to be exact, turned my mourning into dancing for sure. Anyone who says that they are not forever ruined when they become a grandparent just isn't being truthful! It is the best experience, and I wouldn't trade it for the world.

The next trial was when my daughter, now married to the kids' father, moved from Meridian, Mississippi to Texas. It was so hard to have them so far away. I also have two sons that had moved to Iowa, and so when it was time for vacation, I was always torn as to where to go. I was born and raised in Iowa. My extended family lives there and Eric's mother also. Again, I survived. I went and visited as often as I could, and time passed.

While filling in at my husbands store, one of our customers told me some welcome news. They told me that Mississippi had adopted something called the Cottage Food Law which made it legal to operate a baking business from your home without the necessity of having a food license. The rules were strict but doable.

It was at this juncture that I struggled with my insecurities. I had been told many times that I should go into business. But was that wat God wanted me to do? I just had to know. So again, I did as I had learned to do and took it to the Lord in prayer. The idea was exciting to me, but I had no confidence in myself to pull it off. So, I asked the Lord to give me scriptural confirmation.

I am always amazed at how patient and kind God is with us when we are weak in our faith.

It was during a church service that the Lord led me to the scripture for my answer. It wasn't even related to what the pastor was preaching that day. It was, however, totally related to the answer I had been seeking the Lord for as to whether I should launch out into business for myself. The Lord showed me Joshua 1:3 where He promised to give Joshua the ground where his feet trod. The Lord continued to take me all the way through to the 9th verse. In those nine verses, God tells Joshua three times to be strong and of good courage. I took that to mean that God was saying yes to the idea of me starting my own business baking from my home but not to be deceived because it wasn't always going to be easy. That was good enough for me.

The rules were very strict for the Mississippi Cottage Food Law. You could not advertise online or use social media. You couldn't even have a sign in your yard. You had to label all your products with ingredients, allergy alerts, weight, etc. You could only earn so much per year, and on and on went the list. It seemed like a lot, and I was overwhelmed at first, for sure. But I kept plugging away until I got it figured out. I worked out two different routes in our area. So, I would bake on Monday and Tuesday to prepare to go out on my first route on Wednesday. Then on Thursday I would bake to re-stock. I would then go out on my second route on Friday. Soon Ms. Brenda's Baked Goods became familiar around the city. I still have people recognize me, and with kindness, tell me how much they miss my goodies. The first year, to my shock, I had to quit early because I was in danger of going over the income limit for the year. Wow, God was truly blessing me. After expenses, however, I didn't really make much money, and I worked way too many hours, but I gained confidence and people skills. I learned how to charge a proper amount to make at least a little profit. Even my customers told me initially that I wasn't charging enough. I did this for three years until circumstances became such that I needed to consider putting an end to my business at least for a time. This was another decision that I struggled with. After all, God had told me to start this, how could I just quit? I prayed and got God's peace and moved on to helping my daughter with her children so she could work. Her story, while part of mine, is hers to tell. Suffice it to say, that she found herself separated from her husband and in need of help with the children, so I decided it was time for me to stay home and invest in my grandchildren! Did I have reason to worry? Perhaps, but I was finally beginning to realize the futility of such behavior and took God's directive to heart. I often said, out loud "Lord, I trust you with my daughter and grandchildren's future. You are in control. You've got this, and you've got them! I know you do!" Then I did my best to leave it there and not allow anxious thoughts to captivate my mind. I had finally found a way to rest in the Lord during difficult times. I realized that me being anxious was not part of God's perfect plan for His kids. He would have us to rest in him. Doesn't it say somewhere in scripture that His yoke is easy, and His burden is light? He wants to do the hard stuff and let us rest. That's how much He loves us. The problem is we want to try and carry things never intended for us to carry. Isn't it foolish how we try to "help" God answer our prayers? Please understand that I am not saying that we do nothing. We need to be active in our prayers over the struggles of life. The difference is we come to God from a lifestyle of trust rather than coming to Him in desperation. We all have friends or family members in crisis at some point. So, while resting in the fact that the Lord is in control, we need to actively bring our loved ones before the Lord. Instead of anguished cries for God's intervention, we should lift them before the Lord. I often say something like, "Thank you Lord for being with _____! I know that you are working in (his/her) life, and I trust you with (him/her)!" Sometimes I will be directed to pray for something more specific, and I am careful to do so. Afterward I pray for those around them like their spouse and children. I ask God to continue to watch over them, guarding their hearts and minds in Christ Jesus! Then I do my best NOT to worry. If I find myself trying to worry, I say again, "Thank you Lord that you are taking care of (him/her) and their family! I trust you!"

> *Come to me, all you who are weary and*
> *burdened, and I will give you rest.*
> *29. Take my yoke upon you and learn from*
> *me, for I am gentle and humble in heart,*
> *and you will find rest for your souls*
> *30. For my yoke is easy and my burden is light.*
> *(Matthew 11:28–30 NIV)*

Ready for our declaration?

**<u>"God, I believe that You are who You say You are and that You'll do what You say You'll do! I choose to put my complete trust in You. You are my hope and my salvation!</u>**

**<u>Today I say YES to You, Jesus!</u>**

## CHAPTER 11

# WHEN TRAGEDY STRIKES

As will happen, time went by too fast. Eric's job was becoming more and more stressful. He was always on call. He never had a day when he didn't have to go into the store. Also, he was promoted to a supervisory position where he had to oversee other stores with very little extra incentive and a lot more headache. It seemed it was time to look for a new job, so we started praying.

Eric looked and looked for the right job. He had some that offered tempting pay but no less stress. As time went on and he wasn't finding the job he wanted, he approached me about looking for a job. He said he would feel better if I could get something to tide us over, "just in case." Since my grandkids were in school by this time, I was free to look for a job.

In June of 2018, I was offered a job with a bank. Though I had never worked at a bank, I had handled money as a cashier and manager for the fast food store. On the second interview, they offered me the job. I didn't realize that they had irregular hours. Can you believe they were open from 7 a.m. to 7 p.m. Monday through Friday and 9 a.m. to Noon on Saturdays? I wanted to refuse the job then and there, but I felt the strong admonition of the Lord to take the job, so I said yes. Our schedule was indeed unpredictable!! One day I would work from 7 a.m. to 3 or 3:30 p.m. The next day, I might work 11 a.m. to 7 p.m. Then we rotated and usually worked at least one Saturday a month. This kind of schedule makes it hard to plan ahead for trips, or appointments. We rarely knew our schedule more than a week ahead.

While I didn't understand much of the things I was experiencing, looking back I can say that I know at least one reason why God brought me to this bank. He wanted to shed His Holy light on an area of my life that was holding me back from living the life He wanted for me. You see, I lived in constant fear of messing up. I didn't even realize the fear was there until I came to the bank. I was constantly anxious about making mistakes. I mean, this is people's money we are talking about, after all! The truth is, I did make mistakes. Unfortunately, that is how I seem to learn best. I did learn however, and eventually became a decent tell. I was even promoted to Senior teller 😊.

Okay so, about that fear mentioned earlier, here's the rest of the story. I was on the praise and worship team at church. The day came when the worship pastor was going to be out, and he asked me to fill in for him. This shouldn't be a big deal, right? I have led worship before, right? Well, I was petrified!! I was so afraid I was going to mess up and let the Worship Pastor and senior Pastor down, or at least that is what I told myself. As it turned out, I was able to lead worship passingly well and the church survived (Ha!). It was shortly thereafter, during a time at the altar, that the Holy Spirit began to deal with me about this issue. He helped me to realize that my FOMU (Fear of messing up) was really a spirit of fear with a lot of pride mixed in there!! I needed to come to terms with the fact that whether a worship service that I happen to be leading goes well or not isn't up to me. My job is to prepare myself, and it's God's job to do the rest.

> *I have strength for all things in Christ Who empowers*
> *me [I am ready for anything and equal to anything*
> *through Him Who infuses inner strength into me;*
> *I am self-sufficient in Christ's sufficiency].*
> *(Philippians 4:13 AMPC)*

For me to think otherwise is simple pride. I was afraid of looking bad. The spirit of fear was not difficult to deal with once it was exposed. Now, every time I have anxious thoughts about messing up, I simply thank the Lord for helping me to do my best and acknowledge that He is in control! Then I tell the devil to go fly a kite and leave me alone, because I am a child of God and He gives me strength to do all things well!! Now I began to understand why the Lord had led me to the bank. I was able to shake off the fear and apply myself to the job. I still made mistakes, but I tried to learn from them and shake off any fear the enemy was trying to lay on me.

My husband finally landed a great job in October 2018. He got a job working on the Navy base for a contractor doing work similar to what he did on active duty. His starting pay would be twice what he had been making before. He would be working the early shift Monday through Friday with no phone calls on the weekends. What a blessing! We were so excited. Truth is, I could have quit my job right then and there, but I knew God had me there for a reason. So, I stayed where I was.

It wasn't too long before a spot opened at a branch of the bank less than a mile from my house. I was so happy when they offered me the job!! Now my hours would be 8:30 a.m. to 4:30 p.m. Monday through Thursday and 8:30 a.m. to 5:30 p.m. on Fridays. I still had to rotate in for the Saturday shift at the other bank though.

Things were going great until we got a call on a Sunday night after church from our youngest son, informing us that our oldest son, Patrick had been in a serious accident and was in ICU.

We called our pastor and told him what had happened. We were so blessed and surprised when he and his wife showed up at the house to pray with us, even though it was late. Thank God for a caring shepherd!!

Early the next morning, we were on our way north. After we arrived we wasted no time going into the ICU to see him. It was overwhelming to see my son in a brace with the screws going into his head. My head started to spin, and I grabbed the person next to me and said, "I think I am going to faint." The next thing I knew I was waking up on the floor.

Patrick had been thrown from his truck and apparently landed on his neck which was broken. There were tubes everywhere, including one going down his throat and a trachea tube in his neck to help him breathe.

The doctors took us into a room and explained that Patrick had injuries to his neck and spinal cord. They didn't give us much hope that he would walk again. When we expressed our faith in God to heal Patrick they were quick to caution us not to get our hopes up.

It was a long week! We prayed and prayed. I remember reading to him and trying to talk to him, feeling so helpless! I know he felt helpless too, not being able to communicate. The church was good to us, of course. They even brought a bag full of snacks and journals, among other things. What a blessing!!

I cried when the week was up because we had to return to Mississippi. By this time, Patrick was able to talk as they had removed the tube from his neck. He was in good spirits, always joking around. Once I asked him if he needed anything. Even before he could talk, using the computer they had given him to help him communicate, he responded with, "a million bucks!"?

I went back to work praying always, and Patrick was eventually released to physical therapy in the town closer to his home. He had been at the University Hospital about an hour away from where I grew up and further from where Patrick lived at the time. Patrick was paralyzed from the neck down and his hands and fingers did not function properly due to his neck injury.

I made a daily habit of calling Patrick to check on him. I helped him from afar as much as I could. He always kept his chin up and kept his eyes on God. I am proud of him for that!! About a week after I had been back to work, I got a call from Patrick. He exclaimed that he was able to move his right toe 😊! I was so excited, I wanted to do a dance! I just knew that God was going to heal him completely and soon!!

The accident happened in November of 2018. As of today, Patrick can move his right leg some but still cannot use his hands properly and is still in a wheelchair. We are still believing for a miracle but meanwhile I am trusting God to do a complete work in my son. I knew that God wanted to do some things in Patrick and have been as patient as I know how.

Since the accident, Patrick has worked himself out of the need for social security. He works transporting medical patients for a contractor. He is a gifted young man when it comes to people! He never met a stranger, and he has the ability to love people that most would overlook or dismiss on general principles. All I know to say is, God's not finished with him yet! Occasionally, when I am praying for him, I will say, "Lord, what about today? It would be a great day to heal Patrick don't you think?" I always think of the little guy in the movie *Angels in the Outfield*. He kept saying, "It could happen!" He got his angel, and I firmly believe Patrick will get his miracle! Meanwhile, we will continue to be faithful with what He has given us!

From here, my story turns back to my daughter. She had established herself here in Mississippi and was doing well, renting a house from her father-in-law while still separated from her husband, who was still in Texas. She called and asked if she could move back in temporarily because her father-in-law and his family were moving back to Panama and needed to do something with the house. So, we agreed. This would give her time to find a place of her own again, which isn't easy in this area.

Before she was ready to move in, she got Covid in October of 2020. She went to a hospital in Alabama, where her sister-in-law worked, to get an infusion. Apparently, she passed out in the ER. For whatever reason, they did x-rays of her lungs and were about to send her home when two nurses insisted they take another look. God used these two ladies to help them detect a problem.

Finally, I got a call from Erica, who was on her way home from the hospital, saying she had something she needed to tell us and asking if she could come over. Remember, she had COVID. We figured it must be important, so we agreed. When she arrived, she came in, and, sitting as far away from us as she could, she told us that the nurses at the hospital detected something in an X-ray that indicated she might have a serious medical issue. The word cancer wasn't spoken but certainly implied. We prayed with her and encouraged her to trust the Lord. As it turns out, she did have cancer, specifically Hodgkins Lymphoma. We continued praying and believing for God's healing.

She moved back in with us in February of 2021. I was truly happy that I could be there to help her with the kids.

It was heartbreaking when my daughter called and said, "Momma, they said I'm going to lose my hair." We cried together, and I did my best to encourage her to keep her trust in the Lord. He was going to get her through this.

The other difficult thing the doctors had to say was that because of the chemotherapy treatment she would have to endure, she would most likely no longer be able to have children. This was difficult to hear!

I did what I could to encourage my daughter. I reminded her that with God, all things are possible. I told her about a friend of ours who went through chemotherapy and was told the same thing who now has a beautiful baby boy. My prayers continued to be: "Lord, I trust You with my daughter's future! Father, preserve that part of her body that produces children, in Jesus' Name!"

So, the treatment finally began. Even though I was working, I did my best to go to treatments with her so she wouldn't be alone.

I prayed for her when she was getting sick in the bathroom. My husband would pick the kids up from school when needed. We did everything we could to help her.

When her hair began to fall out, she decided to shave it off. Then she had fun purchasing wigs she could wear. She even had a blue green one. I love the fact that she had such a great attitude! Meanwhile, I was praying that when her hair grew back it would be just like she had always wanted it to be: Straight, thick, black and not frizzy!

Time passed, she continued going to her treatments, eventually telling me she really didn't need me to come with her. I had to respect that since she takes her independent nature from me. The day finally came when they tested her and declared that she was in remission.

The clinic where she received her treatment had a bell that you got to ring when you were finally cancer-free. It was a happy day when Erica got to ring that bell!!

I am happy to report that Erica's hair has grown back wavy and not frizzy. Previously her hair had been very curly, thin, brown, and frizzy. I thought it was beautiful, but it wasn't what she wanted. It grew back thicker, curly, and darker but not black. Anyway, she got part of her wish. Either way, it grew back super cute! Her curls, she declared, would not cooperate, saying, "They do whatever they want, I can't control them."

Erica has acquired the same joy and talent that I have for baking. She is better than I am in many ways. With no fear, she plowed into a business of her own selling baked goods. One of her first endeavors was making cheesecake, which anyone who bakes knows is no easy task. On her first try, she made four different cheesecakes, using her artistic skill. They were a big hit. She has perfected her cheesecakes now and sells them often. That may not have much to do with our topic, but I had to brag a little 😊.

Again, time went on. Erica continued to get her health back. Her divorce became final, and she could now move on with her life. This is one of those bittersweet things. I do believe that divorce is always a sad thing but, in this case, it needed to happen for Erica to be able to move on. It had been nearly five years since they had separated. He had moved on, and it was time for her to do the same.

Ironically, she became close to our best friends' son. They became an item. They had known each other for years. In fact, they grew up in church together. Now they were dating. The day came when her boyfriend even came and asked my husband for his blessing before planning an elaborate proposal. They enjoyed going to escape rooms together with friends, so he planned an escape room experience to remember. At the end, she was led to a ring box, and he proposed to her with all their friends as witnesses.

Meanwhile, his mother and I were busy setting up an after- party to include homemade Pizza. So, we had a feast ready for all of us to celebrate with them.

Now comes my favorite part. They are married and God performed the miracle we had prayed for during her battle with cancer. As I write this, Erica has just given birth to the most beautiful baby boy! He is still just days old. I am especially thankful to the Lord for showing my daughter how much he loves her. Perhaps it has helped her to trust Him just a little bit more herself.

*Yes, though I walk through the [deep sunless]*
*valley of the shadow of death, I will fear or dread*
*no evil, for You are with me; Your rod [to protect]*
*and Your staff [to guide], they comfort me.*
*Psalms 23:4 (AMPC)*

Ready for our declaration?

**"God, I believe that You are who You say You are and that You'll do what You say You'll do! I choose to put my complete trust in You. You are my hope and my salvation!**

**Today I say YES to You, Jesus!**

## CHAPTER 12

# DOUBLE PORTION

I have spoken a lot about my mother and her giftings. I want to take some time to revisit this point again. Did I mention that my mother and a friend of hers started a weekly prayer group years ago? They had a group of folks that would come. They would start their meeting just talking about their week. Then they would talk about prayer needs. Often my mom's friend, Wanda, would give a message in tongues and my mom would interpret. One of their goals was to teach folks how to properly use the gifts of the Holy Spirit mentioned in 1 Corinthians 12.

Whenever I visited, if possible, I would join them for this meeting. It was always one of those things that half scared me, but I felt drawn to be a part of it because I knew my mother and could not deny the veracity of it. Ms. Wanda has since gone on to be with the Lord, but my mother continues to lead this group.

Once, in recent years, during my private prayer time at home, I felt like the Lord had challenged me to ask him for a double portion of my mother's anointing. I wrestled with that Idea for a while, but I finally did as he directed.

The next time I was attending one of my mom's prayer meetings, my mother put me in the "chair". This was a special seat where you sat to be prayed for regarding specific needs. She said the Lord was about to give me that double portion I had asked for. They prayed for me and honestly, I didn't feel any different. However, I accepted the truth that God had given me that double portion. After all, He was the one who told me to ask for it, right?

Literally, years went by, and I simply didn't feel any different. Occasionally I would ask the Lord about it. I truly wanted to be able to interpret a message in tongues but when one was given, I heard nothing. Call me a coward if you want, but I wasn't about to just start talking and hope the Lord would give me the words. I always want to be authentic. I don't want to be one of those problem people we talked about earlier, right?

One day when I was talking to the Lord about this issue, He told me that He had given me the double portion that I had asked for. However, it was not going to look like I had imagined. I took that to mean that I could not expect God to use me exactly as He has used my mother. While I might interpret messages in tongues or prophesy, God, perhaps, had a different plan for me. My job was to trust Him and let the Holy Spirit teach me. Presently, I am still learning what that looks like, but I am indeed trusting Him along the way. Again, I find myself infinitely grateful for God's patience with His kids!

This is a short segment but is relevant to the next step in my journey so stay with me 😊.

> *He who did not withhold or spare [even] His own*
> *Son but gave Him up for us all, will He not also with*
> *Him freely and graciously give us all [other] things?*
> *Romans 8:32 AMPC*

Ready for our declaration?

**"God, I believe that You are who You say You are and that You'll do what You say You'll do! I choose to put my complete trust in You. You are my hope and my salvation!**

**Today I say YES to You, Jesus!**

## CHAPTER 13

# BUT FOR THE GRACE OF GOD, THERE GO I

During all the time my daughter was dealing with cancer treatments, etc. I was still working at the bank, wishing I could just stay home and take care of her. I would pray and ask the Lord about it, but I kept getting the same answer. I was to stay put until He released me. One time, the Lord said something like "I will soon release you from this job, but it will not look like you have imagined."

Have you ever watched someone go through an ordeal like Cancer and wondered how you would handle such an experience if it happened to you? Over the years I have watched many people that I care for go through tough times. I have even prayed something like, "Oh Lord, that I might be able to walk through such a struggle as they are going through with Your grace." While I prayed such prayers many times, I never really expected to actually have to face anything like the things other people I knew had experienced. I mean, bad things like that happen to other people, right?

While I was busy working at the bank, I noticed some weird things going on with my eyes. I thought it was my glasses because I was having a terrible time getting them adjusted to fit correctly. I am one of those people who do not like to go to the doctor about every little thing, because I know it might lead to a long series of tests and things no one really enjoys. So, I just kept ignoring the "little" things. Also, I had been developing a lifestyle of trusting the Lord and wanted to be led by Him, not a doctor.

One day, as I thought about one of those small issues, I said a simple prayer: "Lord, if there is something that needs to be addressed medically, would you bring it to light? Otherwise, I am simply going to trust you to take care of me."

Not long after that prayer one Saturday, my husband and I decided to take a trip to Sam's, which we did almost religiously every weekend. We were getting ready, you know, getting presentable for a public appearance. Quite suddenly, I developed a headache. Headaches are not unusual for me, especially with pollen or weather changes that always seem to cause headaches for me. I remember saying, "Man, my head really hurts." Eric asked if we needed to stay home, but I was sure it would pass, so we headed out.

It was not fine, however. By the time we arrived at Sam's (about a 15-minute drive), I was feeling nauseous and when Eric stopped to get gas, I asked him to find me something I could use in case I needed to vomit. He got me something just in time. Again, he asked if we should go home. I told him we might as well get what we came for since we were there. I stayed in the car and was okay until he returned, but once the car started to move, I got sick again.

We headed home and Eric put me to bed. This was short lived as the headache increased in intensity, and we finally made the decision to go to the ER.

At the hospital they, of course, had to test me for Covid which was negative, and then they gave me some medicine, I don't recall what it was. I soon began to feel better, and I was eventually released to go home.

The hospital suggested that I go and see my family doctor on Monday if I still wasn't feeling better. I stayed home from Church on Sunday, which I almost never do. I figure I can sit at home feeling miserable, or I can go to church where I am among the family that will pray for me. I say that only to help you realize that I really was not feeling well.

Monday morning came, and I called the clinic to find that my doctor was not available, so I made an appointment with the on-call doctor. Then I called work to let them know what was going on with me.

When I saw the doctor that day, He did an X-ray of my sinuses, thinking maybe I had an infection. He sent me home with a prescription for antibiotics and a doctor's excuse to stay home from work until Wednesday. He said if I still wasn't feeling better, to come back.

Wednesday came and I still had a headache although not migraine level, so I called and was able to make an appointment with my regular doctor at 3:15 in the afternoon. She listened as I told her all that had transpired since my trip to the ER. She is one of those doctors that ask you what you would like her to do. This always frustrated me, so I was surprised when she asked, "Has anyone done a CT scan on you?" When I replied, "No," she said she felt like that would be best. Looking back, I can see God's hand even in this little detail. She didn't ask me if I thought we should do it. In fact, she acted with urgency. She called ahead as the place they did the CTs at the hospital was due to close at 4:30.

We hustled to the imaging department at the hospital, and they were ready for us. They took me in and did the CT and after a short wait, they told us we could go. We were heading out the automatic doors when a nurse flagged us down and asked us to please come back, that they needed to talk to us. Again, I see the hand of God preventing a problem that needed to be addressed from being overlooked. So, they sat us down and explained that the CT had revealed a 4.5 cm mass on my brain.

I don't remember a lot from here. I know that my head was hurting massively. They had me on a gurney hooking me up to an IV. I remember the euphoric feeling I had when they administered a medicine called Dilaudid (not sure if I spelled that right), I think. Wow, that stuff was amazing! 😊 I remember thinking that must be what it felt like to be on drugs.

There was a very bad storm in progress that night and they were making plans to transport me to Jackson, which was 90 miles away. I told the doctor that I would prefer my husband to drive me, if possible. He told me that most doctors would not allow this, but he was not one of them. The hand of God had moved again, and we were headed to Jackson in a terrible downpour. I was grateful that Eric, who is an excellent driver, was behind the wheel!!

By the time we got to Jackson, it was late and, of course, we had to check in at the ER and wait forever. When we finally got called, they sent me for another CT or maybe it was an MRI, I don't recall. This confirmed that there was a mass. They, however, estimated it to be more like 5 cm in size.

There were no regular rooms available on the main floors, so I spent an uncomfortable two days, one in the ER room and another in regular ICU. By this time, my oldest son had come down from Iowa to be with me. What a blessing that was to me! I was also blessed to have our pastors and our best friends all there to help support us.

One thing I want to say here, I was at total peace through all of this. It was a supernatural kind of peace. I mean, it's not normal to be totally at peace when you've just been told you have a mass on your brain that very likely is malignant.

The ones struggling the most were my family members I believe. I am so grateful for the support structure we have!

After the night in ICU, I finally was put in a regular room. This was so much more comfortable! Somewhere along the line, we met with a neurosurgeon who explained to us that surgery was necessary. He also explained that the mass was in the vision center of the brain and would affect my vision if it hadn't already. Bottom line, it needed to be removed. As the hand of God continued to move, the doctor asked us if we had a faith, did we "follow

Christ?" My heart soared as I realized that God had put me in the hands of a Christian doctor.

So, surgery was scheduled for the following Monday, two days before our 37th wedding anniversary. They decided it was best for me to stay at the hospital rather than being discharged only to have to return Monday.

The first day in the regular room was kind of miserable. My bowels were backed all the way up and I couldn't go 😖. I know, too much information, but hang with me. God was answering the prayers of His people when he appointed the nursing staff that cared for me. They were all great, but one stood out from the crowd. She prepared me a concoction she called "the brown cow" that finally got me moving (phew). She also told me as they were rolling me out for surgery that she would see me after. True to her word, she was there when I woke in the Neuro ICU. Thank God for her bright smile!

The next couple days went by with normal hospital routine. My best friend stayed with me the first night to give Eric a chance to go home, shower and get some rest.

During this time, I felt led by the Lord to make videos to put on Facebook to let folks know how I was. I honestly do not like putting myself out there like that, but I really felt God's prompting to do so. It ended up being a series of videos over a period of time. I still have people who will tell me how much of a blessing and inspiration I was to them. It is hard to explain the way I felt through all of this. I honestly had complete peace. I had confidence in the doctors because I trusted the Lord.

> *You will guard him and keep him in perfect and constant peace whose mind [both its inclination and its character] is stayed on You, because he commits himself to You, leans on You, and hopes confidently in You.*
> **Isaiah 26:3 MPC**

Here I would like to tell a side story that I think is important. My pastor is fond of saying that God is not surprised when things like what was happening to me occur. So, about a week before all this happened, my mother declared that she felt led by the Lord to get everyone together and have a short praise session. So, she gathered her folks and we gathered ours and we put the phones on speaker, and she led us first in prayer as the Lord had directed her and then she said, "Now, let's just praise the Lord together." And we did. It was a blessing to feel the presence of the Lord bridge the miles and settle on both households. God knew what was coming! This is how I fight my battles!! Have you heard that song?? We were fighting a battle we didn't even know was coming. Thank you Lord for a praying, obedient mother!

The day of surgery finally arrived early Monday morning. I had been praying, and I really wanted to have a time of prayer before surgery. I told Eric and my pastor that I wanted them to be there, and I wanted to get my mom on the phone so we could all agree together. I felt like this was something God put in my heart, while wondering how it would work out. Well, our Christian surgeon came into the room and said, "Okay, are you ready to get this over with?"

We had just talked to our pastor who had called to

let us know that he was on the way, but they had run into traffic and would be another ten minutes. Well, you don't know unless you ask, right? So, I simply asked the surgeon if he would be willing to wait for the pastor to get there. I watched as he hesitated and then agreed. He stepped out of the room and leaned against the wall in the hallway. It was then that I got the sense that God was wanting to do something special in that man's life. It isn't always about us, or at the very least it isn't always only about us. This is a good thing to remember when you are going through tough times. While God IS working in your life, He might also be using your circumstances to work in someone else's life.

Our pastor arrived and I had my mother on the phone, and we prayed together. I had absolutely no fear. I was completely at peace. In fact, I was rejoicing that the doctor agreed to wait for Pastor to get there. Later, Pastor told us that in nearly forty years of ministry, he had never experienced a doctor willing to wait on a preacher to get there and pray over his patient. Don't tell me God wasn't up to something good!

After surgery, Eric told me that the surgeon came and explained to him how the surgery went and that it did look like the worst scenario. He was able to remove only 75-85% of the tumor. The doctor did his best to encourage him. He told Eric that they sent a sample for testing and that the pathology report would tell us more. Once again, I am so thankful for my church family! Eric broke down, surrounded by the pastor and our closest friends. He was in a safe place to be human, to be weak, and to let others be strong for him without judgment. When I heard this part of his story, I realized that in many ways, the whole ordeal was more difficult for him than it was for me. I was the one experiencing God's supernatural peace. Eric was struggling.

The next two days I was in the Neuro ICU. I tell people that those two days were the worst and the best two days of my stay at the hospital and truly my entire experience. I woke in a dark room and could not see anything. I couldn't find a comfortable position. I couldn't find my phone or my glasses. I was thirsty but couldn't find a call button to get help. I felt completely vulnerable and helpless! I would drift off into wonderful sleep only to be awakened by the nurses out in the other room chatting away, while I was frustrated and needing their help. That was the hard part of the experience.

On the other side, I guess while I was sleeping or perhaps it really was a vision, I cannot tell, but God showed me some really cool stuff. First, it was as if I was looking down on myself. I could see a hand holding a pitcher like they would serve water from at a restaurant. This pitcher, however, did not hold water. It contained a florescent substance that looked like glow-in-the dark liquid. The hand that held the pitcher was pouring this substance over me from my head to my toes. Again, I don't know how I came to this conclusion, but I understood this to be the Double Portion that I spoke of earlier, the one God had challenged me to ask for. The truth is, God was indeed doing a work in me. I emerged from this experience with a boldness and confidence to share God's word with folks that I have never had. I was experiencing direction from the Lord that I never questioned; I just knew.

The other dream or Vision was a picture of what was happening and what was going to happen in my brain.

I envisioned a massive construction site. To the left there were tables where the engineers were poring over blueprints. The rest of the site looked like a beehive of workers busily putting me back together as if a storm had damaged a building and they were rebuilding it. One of my favorite parts was when this funny guy, who I figured was a foreman, came across the forefront of my vision. He had a bundle of wiring over one shoulder that he was hauling somewhere, when he stopped and points at one of the workers and said something like, "Hey, George, stop right there! What do you think you are doing? That doesn't go there. Have you even been to the engineer's table to get your instructions? Come on, people, we can't afford to get this wrong. It's too important!"

Then the vision focused upwards to, maybe, a second floor. The light was bright and there were workers pulling everything out. They were gutting the whole area. I came to understand that this was the vision center of my brain. The Spirit of the Lord spoke to me right then. It wasn't an audible voice, but I knew Who was speaking to me. He said something like, "They are removing everything so they can prepare for the new equipment. This will take time. They must put in the hardware to receive modern technology. Also, some of the modern technology isn't even ready for distribution yet. You will be getting the top of the line, the most up-to-date technology possible.

New Eyes." I took that as a promise that I have held on to. When this is all said and done, I won't need my glasses!

The second day in the Neuro ICU they took me to the imaging department for CT and MRI testing where they use dye for contrast. Later, the surgeon's assistant came in smiling to report that according to the results of the testing they had just done, the surgeon was mistaken in his original assessment. In fact, he had been able to remove 90-95% of the tumor! God continued to work!!

Two days after surgery, we celebrated our anniversary with our best friends, bringing in food from one of our favorite Italian Restaurants in the area. We ate together in the cafeteria while we waited to be discharged officially.

It felt great to be home and able to sleep in my own bed. This was Wednesday and I was so anxious to see my church family. However, my sweet husband was exhausted, so we stayed home. Sunday church was a blessing!! There is no place like home!! That includes my church home!!

One of the first things I was able to do was bake! God was gracious to me. He knew my passion and I needed to be able to assure myself that I could still do what I love. So, a couple of weeks after being home and learning how to navigate without completely good eyesight, I made three different kinds of batter bread, the recipes of which I knew by heart and didn't need to read.

Now, let's discuss my eyesight. You may be thinking that God said he was going to heal them. You would be right; He did say that. However, He didn't say when. So, I was dealing with blurred vision overall, as well as a blockage in my left field of vision. I thought it was only in my left eye, but the ophthalmologist visit confirmed that there was a blockage in the left field of vision for both eyes :

I was not legally able to drive because of it. Wow, that was hard to hear. Anyone who knows me knows that I am very independent and being stuck at home having to rely on other people is not easy for me, to say the least!

Eric took me back for our follow-up appointments with the Pathologist. We were excited about the first appointment because we were hoping to hear the results of the pathology report. Unfortunately, the pathology report had not been handed down yet. My pathologist encouraged me by saying that this was actually good news. She said that when the news was bad, the reports came in very quickly. The fact that they were taking so long was encouraging to her way of thinking. She then proceeded to tell us what we might expect in the days to come. She spoke of radiation treatment and chemotherapy in the form of a pill that I would take monthly. This all depended on the official report, of course.

For the first time, I became a little overwhelmed and had my first tears over the situation. I was not suddenly afraid I was going to die. Rather, I had become overwhelmed with the uncertainty of my immediate future: radiation treatment, chemotherapy, what should I tell my work? All these thoughts were bombarding my peace. Not knowing is hard for most people and for a brief moment, I was indeed overwhelmed. Perhaps I needed that release of emotion? Anyway, Eric and I prayed, and I know family and friends were praying also, and my peace soon returned.

The next time I returned to the hospital it was for a

follow-up appointment with the surgeon. We were happy to find that he had the pathology report in hand. We were able to walk it down to my pathologist, as her office was in the same building.

The report indeed was the biggest reason to praise yet. The diagnosis was downgraded from stage 4 cancer to a **Low grade ependymoma centered in the occipital lobe**. This was huge news. This meant that the death sentence the enemy tried to lay on me was off the table, at least as far as I was concerned. This also meant that it was much more treatable than previously thought! My pathologist told us that further MRI testing showed there was only 5% of the tumor remaining, and I would need to have radiation treatment to make sure it doesn't come back. However, chemotherapy would not be necessary with the new diagnosis!

It amazes me how God works. I remembered when my daughter was going through treatment. After she had completed her chemotherapy treatments, her doctor suggested radiation treatment for her. I could only advise, but as I prayed about it, I felt an unrest that made me think it was NOT a good idea. I shared my concerns with Erica and continued to pray that God would help her make the right decision. She eventually decided not to do radiation. Now here I was in a similar situation, but I had complete peace and confidence that this doctor knew what she was doing. Remember, I had told the Lord in my prayers that I trusted the doctors because I trusted Him. I asked him to show me if something they were suggesting wasn't part of His plan; otherwise, I would follow their plans for me.

So, after some frustration and delays, I finally was able

to contact the radiologist and set an appointment to get the ball rolling for treatment. It was a blessing that he was local so I wouldn't have to drive ninety miles to get treatment. This was especially good since I had thirty-three treatments spread over six weeks ahead of me. The next hurdle was to figure out how to get there and back. My husband, now out of leave time, had to go back to work. He was gone from the house by 4 a.m. each day so if he were to take me, it would have to be in the afternoon. I really wanted to get it over with early in the day, so I started praying. I truly felt that there was someone in our church community that needed a project, so to speak. I have an amazing church family and we found a young man who works at the church who would be willing to take me.

We often go with our best friends to his mom's house for dinner on Sunday after church. We were sitting in the dining room discussing the issues with getting me to treatment when Mom Smith, as I call her, said, "I could take you." I was surprised by this as she was in her eighties and my experience with older people is that usually they are slow moving in the morning. I cautioned her that treatment would begin at 7:30 a.m. every morning, Monday through Friday, for six weeks. She said that was just fine with her, as she was an early riser anyway. so, I told her that I would let the young man from church take me the first time, since it was already set up, and then she could take over from there. It turned out to be such a blessing! I enjoyed getting the chance to get to know Mom Smith better, and she said she was blessed to have a project to keep her busy and getting to know me was an added bonus for her as well.

So, I went through treatment with virtually no issues. I did lose hair at the treatment site but because I have very thick hair, I was able to comb my hair at the top of my head over the affected area and no one really knew that I had a hidden bald spot😊. I would arrive and they would take me back almost immediately. The treatment took only about ten minutes once I was all settled on their little table. The staff was super, and I was thankful!

## GOD'S PERFECT TIMING

Let's talk about God's perfect timing. One of the "what-if's" and "How will this work out?" problems was a fishing trip we had planned months in advance of this whole experience. My big brother and son and granddaughter were going to come from Iowa. Erica was going to watch my granddaughter while we went on an overnight fishing trip. We had reserved a flat boat that Patrick would easily be able to roll his wheelchair onto. My concern was how I could work this in around my treatment schedule. We discussed it with the radiologist. They said that we would have to skip a couple treatments. This was not ideal, but they would work with me. It turned out that, due to a lack of communication, the treatment was delayed and hadn't started by the time we were to go on our trip.

Each time I would be tempted to worry about the timing of the trip, I would say aloud something like, "Lord, thank you for working out the timing of this fishing trip! I know you are working on it, and I trust you!"

Because of the delay in treatment, we were able to

make that fishing trip with no worries or complications. We had a wonderful time!

The fishing charter was on a Tuesday. We went out to eat after a day of fishing and spent the night in a hotel. We headed home on Wednesday. Thursday morning, I finally got the name of the radiologist referred to me and gave him a call. They said they had some paperwork for me to fill out and return, then they would set up a time for us to discuss treatment. Friday morning, I got a call from them saying they had a cancelation. They asked if it would be possible for me to come in that afternoon at 1:30 p.m. Since I wasn't allowed to drive, I called my husband. He was able to get off work early to help me keep that appointment. So, the timing worked out just right.

I was also anxious about my work. I didn't know what to tell them when they asked when I would be able to return. I had no definitive answer for them. Also, the bank afforded me very good benefits. They were working with me. First, I had to use all my leave time. Then I was able to apply for help from a "leave pool" where I had previously donated my own time. I also had an issue with the timing of the Long-Term Disability benefit that was available to me. The catch was I had to be off work for ninety days before I would qualify. As it turned out, I ran out of FMLA leave on May 5th, just days after the ninety days were up. I received my last paycheck on May 19th. All the paperwork for long-term disability was completed and I did qualify, Praise the Lord!! It kicked in and I received my first disability check on June 2nd. It was 60% of my original pay. Once again, God had everything covered, and I was anxious for no reason. God was teaching me to rest in His timing.

> 1)*He who dwells in the secret place of the Most High shall remain stable and fixed under the shadow of the Almighty [Whose power no foe can withstand].*
> 2) *I will say of the Lord, He is my Refuge and my Fortress, my God; on Him I lean and rely, and in Him I [confidently] trust!*
> 3) *For [then] He will deliver you from the snare of the fowler and from the deadly pestilence.*
> 4) *[Then] He will cover you with His pinions, and under His wings shall you trust and find refuge; His truth and His faithfulness are a shield and a buckler.*
> **Psalms 91:1-4 AMPC**

Ready for our declaration?

**"God, I believe that You are who You say You are and that You'll do what You say You'll do! I choose to put my complete trust in You. You are my hope and my salvation!**

**Today I say YES to You, Jesus!**

## CHAPTER 14

# THE BATTLE

I said that I had been walking in perfect peace. While I was enjoying it, I couldn't help wondering how long it would last. I have said that I am naïve, but I realized that the enemy of my soul would not let me go without challenge.

One challenge was my sleep pattern. Because of the steroids I was prescribed, I would find myself wide awake at 1:30 a.m. At first, I struggled to go back to sleep. Meanwhile, my mind was full of God speaking to me about different things. Before I knew it, I was getting up and writing down things the Lord was telling me He wanted me to do. One prominent thing I have already mentioned was making videos to post on Facebook. I do not like doing such things, but I was obedient, and I still hear people saying how much of a blessing those videos were to them. So, God took what the enemy meant for evil and turned it around for my good.

Another big challenge came the weekend before our big fishing trip. I always spend a lot of time in the kitchen preparing food when my family comes to visit. I try to do things ahead so I can spend my time with them while they are here instead of being in the kitchen the whole time. So, Friday night while they were traveling through the night, I was making my son's favorite breakfast casserole so I could get up early and pop it into the oven and have breakfast ready when they arrived. I was down to adding milk to the eggs and had to open a new gallon of milk. There is a seal under the lid that is always so hard to pull off with your hands, right? So, what did I do? I used my teeth. Every time I am tempted to do that now, I can hear my dentist's words, "Teeth are not tools." Well, as I bit down on the little tab that you are supposed to pull with your fingers, my front teeth, in the form of a bridge, came out instead. There I am watching in horror as my teeth bounce across the counter. My first thought was, "Oh no! I am on the worship team on Sunday, AND I am supposed to lead a song!" Looking in the mirror, I looked like a kid who had lost her two front teeth, except there were two spikes where my bridge had been attached. I had to laugh when my grandson, who didn't know what had happened said, "Nanny, why do you look like a vampire?" 😊

We tried everything to find a temporary fix since the dentist would not be available to help me until Monday. Nothing worked. Yes, I did check the internet. I tried suggestions from YouTube to no avail.

I contacted our worship leader to let him know what was going on. I told him I thought I had a plan that would work but wanted to wait until Sunday morning to try lest I mess it up during the night. I am just stubborn enough that I did not want to give the enemy the satisfaction of keeping me out of church and away from my privilege of helping with worship.

Sunday morning arrived and my plan fell apart. I could not get anything to hold my teeth in place, even temporarily. I went to church anyway; I just resisted the urge to smile a lot like I usually do. I talked with our worship pastor as well as our senior pastor and we came up with the plan. We would keep this on the "down low," as the saying is. The fewer people that knew, the better. I told my worship pastor that if he agreed, I would like to stay on the worship team. I felt that if I kept my microphone in front of my mouth no one would be the wiser. Also, the less focus on me the better. So, I suggested that perhaps someone else should lead the song I was supposed to lead.

I felt like I gave the devil a black eye that day. He failed in his plan to keep me out of church, and he did not steal my joy!

I was learning to keep my eyes on God and trust that He had a plan for every circumstance of my life, good or bad. He has my back!! Thank you, Lord!

*We demolish arguments and every pretension that sets itself up against the knowledge of God, and we take captive every thought to make it obedient to Christ.*
*2 Corinthians 5:10 NIV*

These are just a couple more obvious examples of how the enemy tries to derail the plans God has for us. There were days that I struggled with my emotions. Frustration over my limitations was a temptation to fuss and complain.

When I realize that I am drifting that way, I must stop and "bring that thought captive to the obedience of Christ." (2 Corinthians 10:5) This takes an act of determination on our part. We must decide that we do not want to allow the enemy to control our emotions nor our thought life. This gets easier with practice. This reminds me of an important principle I learned from a friend. She was teaching at our Women's Group at church. She described a train where there were three cars. The engine was called Faith. The second car was called Action, and the Caboose was called Feeling. Many times, we must act by Faith. Part of trusting God is being obedient even when we don't understand, even when we can't see what the result will be, or when we just aren't feeling it. So, first, we take God at His word, then we act in obedience to God's direction, then the feeling we were looking for will come. This is how faith and trust grow. You see, without that middle car (action) you don't really have a train. Faith without works is dead, right? (James 2:26).

Lest I bore you with too many details, let me simply say that I have had my good days and my days of struggle. Overall, I have been able to keep my eyes on God. He has blessed me with so many wonderful people who are still praying for me.

My daughter has, and still does, call me often offering to take me somewhere or inviting me to go with her somewhere. Now that the baby is here, she has only to stop by and let me hold him and my day is made!!

I have even been able to connect with a group of people willing to allow me to play the ever-popular sport of pickleball. Sometimes, I lose a ball in that blocked field of vision, but I praise God that I can be active! And He has placed me with a group of people to play with that are gracious to me. Instead of not wanting to play with me, they are always encouraging me.

I have brought you to my current state of being. I am still not able to see well enough to be legal to drive. I am still having follow-up appointments with doctors. I still have my good days and my not-so-good days. The good news is that I still have family and a church full of people who are standing with me in faith. All I need to do is pick up the phone and someone is there to assist me with whatever I need. Meanwhile, I spend my days, working on projects that I set for myself, like writing books 😊 . I am doing the work to put together that cookbook that I always said I was going to do for my daughter and other family members. I even used my rotary sander and dusted off paint drippings from a floor we are planning on refinishing sometime soon. My motto is "I can do ALL things through Christ who strengthens me." When I am feeling down, I must humble myself and ask folks to be strong for me where I am struggling. I keep saying, "Lord, I believe that You are who You say You are and that You will do what You say You will do! I choose to trust you completely! You are my hope and my salvation!"

> **8) Be alert and of sober mind. Your enemy the devil prowls around like a roaring lion looking for someone to devour.**

*9) Resist him, standing firm in the faith, because you know that the family of believers throughout the world is undergoing the same kind of sufferings.*

*10) And the God of all grace, who called you to his eternal glory in Christ, after you have suffered a little while, will himself restore you and make you strong, firm and steadfast.*
*1 Peter 5:8-10 NIV*

Your turn, are you ready?

**"God, I believe that You are who You say You are and that You'll do what You say You'll do! I choose to put my complete trust in You. You are my hope and my salvation!**

**Today I say YES to You, Jesus!**

## CHAPTER 15

# RELATIONSHIP

All that I have shared with you so far comes from my perspective only. It is God who will fill in the blanks for each of you individually because of who He is. As I have been praying about this book, God made one thing clear to me and I want to pass this important point along.

***Trust is born out of relationship.***

If you are reading this book, it is likely that you call yourself a Christian, that is, a follower of Christ. There are many who would label themselves so but do not truly have a relationship with God.

Let's start by defining the word **relationship:** *The way in which two or more people or groups regard and behave toward each other.* Relationships can be complicated, right? Some people run from relationships because they are too difficult to maintain. Bottom line, a good relationship takes time and patience. Just like marriage, you must invest your time and energy into it if you expect it to last a lifetime. Today, many people are either living separate lives while residing under the same roof or they are choosing to divorce rather than fight to make it work. We live in a world where folks feel like they cannot trust anyone.

The truth is you can't trust someone you do not know. My husband and I have been married 37 years and I have learned to trust him. I know him. We have learned to talk and share our feelings openly. This doesn't happen overnight. It takes time to develop.

What if I woke up every morning and said a simple hello to my husband while going through my morning routine, then said a quick goodbye and headed out the door? When I arrived home, what if again I said a quick hello and headed for my easy chair to spend the rest of the evening watching TV generally ignoring my spouse, while I did whatever I wanted until bedtime came and then it was a quick goodnight and off to sleep I went only to repeat the process the next morning? Would you consider this a healthy relationship built on trust? Of course not! Sadly, this is how many Christians live out their "relationship" with the Lord. Oh, they go to church on Sundays because that's the Christian thing to do. However, when Monday comes, it's back to their normal routine again, which seldom includes God at all.

If we want to truly rest in God and learn to trust him, then we must develop a healthy relationship with Him. We need to spend time each day talking to Him. Spend time listening to Him. Make Him a priority in your life. Ask Him what he thinks about things then listen for Him to reply. Be willing to make yourself vulnerable before

Him. Be willing to allow Him to change who you are now into who He intended for you to be all along.

It's okay to be real with God! I mean, look at David. The Psalms are full of David's complaints, frustration, and downright wrong attitudes. Then he would remember just how good, strong, and caring his God was, and he would pull himself back into alignment with who he knew God to be. Then he was back to praising God and having a right attitude.

If the Christian I have just described is you, don't despair! God loves you and truly wants to draw you into intimate relationship with Him! That is what you were created to do, after all. I want to challenge you to step into God's embrace. Use that Scripture in Psalms 139:23,24 where you open your heart to the Lord and let him clean out every dark, dusty corner. It won't always be comfortable, but, I promise, you will not regret it. The more you allow God to do a transforming work in your life, the more you will walk in victory in every area of your life. Christians like to quote scriptures like, "Resist the devil and he will flee from you." The problem is, there is more to that verse. It reads like this:

> *So be subject to God. Resist the devil*
> *[stand firm against him] and he will flee*
> *from you. James 4:5 AMPC*

We like the idea of the devil having to flee from us, but the condition is our submitting our lives to God. If we are not walking in obedience and in complete surrender, the devil will not be obliged to run from us. On the other hand, if we are submitted to God, we DO have authority over the enemy and we no longer have to put up with his annoyances.

Ready for another one of my mom's analogies? Picture yourself standing under a wide umbrella. You are enjoying the protection that an umbrella provides. It keeps you dry when it is raining. It keeps you free from the harsh effects of the hot sun. It even cools the environment around you. All is good until you see something just outside the area covered by the umbrella that you want. If you give in to that temptation and step out to grasp it, you have just stepped out from the protection that umbrella provided, and you are suddenly attacked by the harsh environment outside its protection.

The same is true for us as Christians. If we stay under the protection that a true relationship with Christ provides, every promise in the Word of God applies to us. If, however, we decide that we want something outside that umbrella of God's protection, we forfeit our right to those promises and must embrace the consequences.

I am far from perfect, I admit. I make mistakes often and must repent before the Lord. Let me be perfectly clear. I am a sinner saved by grace. The good news is, God is gracious, and He knows my heart. He knows my weaknesses and yet He is always right there when I come to myself as the prodigal son did, and He is ready to embrace me once again. I can testify of the goodness of God to His children. I can walk in perfect peace consistently. If I lose my peace, it certainly isn't God who pulled away from me. Rather, it is me who has allowed the enemy to steal my joy, either by outright disobedience or by simple carelessness in not working to maintain my relationship with the Lord.

I have said that relationships take work. There will be times when you must fight to keep your joy and peace. The good news is that you have an arsenal of weapons that you can effectively use against the enemy IF you stay under God's protective umbrella. So, I encourage you to get into the Word of God and learn what weapons are available to you and practice using them until it becomes second nature. You will become efficient at the use of these weapons and maintaining peace and joy will come easier and easier no matter what you might be going through. My experience proves to me that I can go through the valley and survive just fine. If I keep my hand in God's, though I fall, I will not be utterly cast down. He is there ready to give me a hand up.

I have assumed that most folks reading this book are indeed Christians just looking for encouragement in how to trust God. Perhaps, however, there are some who have never had a relationship with the Lord. I don't want to miss the opportunity to invite you into the family! I have said that God wants relationship with you. The choice is always yours. He has already chosen you and is waiting for you to choose Him. It is really a very simply procedure. If you want a relationship with the Lord here is what the Bible says about you:

> *That if thou shalt confess with thy mouth the Lord Jesus, and shalt believe in thine heart that God hath raised him from the dead, thou shalt be saved.*

> *For with the heart man believeth unto*
> *righteousness; and with the mouth*
> *confession is made unto salvation.*
> **Romans 10:9,10 NIV**

Once again, a verbal declaration is very important. If you believe that God is who He says He is and will do what He says He will do, then just talk to Him and tell Him that you want to follow Him. Ask Him to forgive you for the sins of your past. Ask him to teach you how to walk in victory as His child. If you do that, you have taken your first step in trusting God. Your next step is to find a Bible believing church where you can grow with the support of other believers. Finally, start a good habit of reading the word and building your very own relationship with a God who has been seeking you all your life! Welcome to the family!

Ready to join us in our declaration?

**"God, I believe that You are who You say You are and that You'll do what You say You'll do! I choose to put my complete trust in You. You are my hope and my salvation!**

**Today I say YES to You, Jesus!**

# CHAPTER 16
# THE POWER OF PRAYER

We have talked about the importance of a relationship with the Lord. Any good counselor will tell you that good communication is a must in any healthy relationship. The same is true in our relationship with the Lord. Prayer is essential for a healthy relationship with God!

Have you ever had someone ask you what your favorite scripture was? That is often a difficult one to answer. I mean, scripture is filled with so much good stuff, how do you choose, right? Well, for me personally, I can say that while I love the word in general, there are some portions that stand out to me. Many of those favorite scriptures I have already shared with you. Now I would like to share the one I would choose, if I was pressed, as my favorite scripture. It's my favorite because it has to do with the all-important practice of prayer.

*6 Do not fret or have any anxiety about anything, but in every circumstance and in everything, by prayer*

*and petition (definite requests), with thanksgiving,
continue to make your wants know to God.*

*7 And God's peace [shall be yours, that tranquil state
of a soul assured of its salvation through Christ, and
so fearing nothing from God and being content with its
earthly lot of whatever sort that is, that peace] which
transcends all understanding shall garrison and mount
guard over your hearts and minds in Christ Jesus.*

*8 For the rest, brethren, whatever is true, whatever
is worthy of reverence and is honorable and seemly,
whatever is just, whatever is pure, whatever is lovely
and lovable, whatever is kind and winsome and
gracious, if there is any virtue and excellence, if there is
anything worthy of praise, think on, weigh, and take
account of these things [fix your minds on them].
Philippians 4:6–8 AMPC*

This scripture is so full of promise. The first thing that caught my attention years ago was the last part of verse 7 that says God's peace will "garrison and mount guard" over your hearts and minds in Christ Jesus. There is a battle that is fought in our thought life that we must learn to win in order to gain and maintain peace. I personally treasure God's amazing peace. I have decided that I will not live without it now that I have learned how to attain it.

**1**

This scripture tells me that I must pray. I must refuse to worry about anything! I must talk to Jesus consistently and be sure to do it with a grateful heart. So, I am careful to thank God for who He is in my life. If anxious thoughts come, I tell myself, "No, we are not going to worry about that! We are going to trust God with it!" Then I grab a hold of His peace, and I imagine an army of Angels guarding my heart and mind. What a great picture!

Verse 8 is a good reminder of how to maintain your peace as well. If you are following the mandates of verse 6 and 7 then your only job is to govern your thoughts. Your thought life is the devil's playground. It is where he whispers his lies and tries to steer you away from the things of God. I encourage you to be vigilant in governing your thoughts. If a thought comes to you that you know is not godly, simply say NO. Say no to yourself. Say no to the devil who is the author of such thoughts. The next step is to purposefully go down the list in verse 8. What IS true? What is worthy of reverence? What is honorable, seemly? What is just, pure, lovely, and kind? Then I say a prayer for God's help. He will not fail you; I promise!

Speaking of prayer, I have been taught that using scripture as a prayer is very effective. This has proven true in my life. That last part of Verse 7 is something I use as a prayer for my loved ones often, especially my children and grandchildren. I ask God to guard their hearts and minds in Christ Jesus. Because God is omnipresent, He can be near our loved ones when we are miles away. Our worry and anxiety will do them no good, while causing us a world of harm. It can even affect your health. So,

I encourage you to dig into the word of God and find scriptures that you can use as a prayer. Memorize them.

Hide them in your heart. God promises that his word will not return void! Let's look at this scripture:

> ***So is my word that goes out from my mouth; It will not return to me empty but will accomplish what I desire and achieve the purpose for which I sent it."***
> ***(Isaiah 55:11 AMPC).***

What an amazing promise! The Bible IS God's word, so if we use it in our prayers, we can be assured it will accomplish what God intends.

Ready for our declaration?

**"God, I believe that You are who You say You are and that You'll do what You say You'll do! I choose to put my complete trust in You. You are my hope and my salvation!**

**Today I say YES to You, Jesus!**

# CONCLUSION

This brings me to where I am now. I am still waiting for God's promise to heal my eyes completely. That said, I am amazed at just how much I can do with the restrictions I have concerning my eyesight. After nearly a year, I am finally able to drive legally, which has restored my independence. Thank you, Jesus! Reading is still a bit of a struggle because everything is slightly out of focus, but I can read, and I am so thankful. I can stay active playing pickleball with my husband. It took him a while to convince me to try. I was surprised to find that I wasn't as terrible as I expected and, as I said, God put us with an amazing group of people who have been so kind and encouraging to me! They keep telling me I'm getting better and better. So, I have the added bonus of getting back in shape. I am officially off steroids and have already been able to lose some of the weight they caused me to gain! Since I am no longer employed full time, I am available to help my daughter with our newest grandson when she needs it. I still bake all the time and am finding projects around the house that I can do. When once I felt sorry for myself with no motivation to do anything,

I now find myself with more projects than I can manage all at once.

The doctors declared me in "complete remission", and I got to ring the same bell as my daughter. God is so faithful!

I walk in God's amazing peace most of the time. I DO have to fight a battle here and there to maintain His peace, but I am well equipped with experience and support of family and friends to win each battle!

As I find myself at the end of our journey together, I am overwhelmed with my desire to see you blessed beyond measure!! As I type these words, my heart is praying:

- that you also will find your place as a child of God, secure in His love.
- that you find a true relationship with your Heavenly Father!
- that you will keep saying YES to Jesus and reap all the benefits of being a joint heir with Him!!
- that you will allow the Holy Spirit to lead you into all truth!
- That you will be able to truly trust the Lord with all your heart and experience rest and peace that comes only from Him!

One Last reminder of what God has tasked me to impress on anyone who will listen. I shared it at the beginning of this book and want to leave it with you as a parting word:

**If you will willingly submit yourself completely to Him and say YES to Him, He will "Expand your capacity to fit HIS purposes for your life"!**

Keep saying **YES to Jesus**! You won't regret it!

**God Bless You!**

## EPILOGUE

It is with a mixture of Joy and sadness that I feel I should add this last bit of news. My hero in the faith has gone on to be with her Lord. My mother passed from this world February 29, 2024, just past midnight. Even in this, she was an inspiration to me, and I wanted to share this experience to both encourage you and so I can remember.

In January of 2024 Mom was rushed to the hospital due to shortness of breath. The doctors did multiple tests which all came out fine until they finally discovered that a valve in her heart was failing.

I talked to her when she was settled back at home again. She was wearing an oxygen mask to help her breathe. They had established plans for a visit from a hospice nurse once a week. She shared her experience at the hospital with unexpected excitement. She said that the doctors wanted her to have surgery, which she refused. She had heart surgery some years ago and she was not keen on doing it again. She told me that the doctors told my brother that they predicted that the valve in her heart would fail within six months. I wish you could have heard the enthusiasm in her voice as she shared this with me. If you didn't know better, you would have thought she was planning a trip to Hawaii. ☺ The point is, she was ready to go and spend eternity with her savior.

A couple weeks after this, my daughter and her children and I made a trip to Iowa so they could see Grandma. It was a tough trip, as we were driving into an Iowa blizzard. We had to stop about an hour and a half short of our destination because the snow was blowing so hard we couldn't see to drive, and the road was covered with ice and snow. We did, however, arrive safely the next day. I was able to add a picture of Mom holding her newest great grandson to my collection.

When we got back to Mississippi, I took a trip with my husband to celebrate our 38th anniversary and then came back and started making plans to return to Iowa to spend more time with my mom in March.

I got a call from my brother soon after our trip saying that the hospice nurse told him that she was thinking Mom had about a month before she would be gone, based on her current condition. I felt prompted to call Mom and tell her that as much as I wanted more time with her, I didn't want her to feel like she had to wait on me. Her response was typical of her. She said, "Well, if I don't see you before, I will see you in Glory".

It wasn't but a week later I got another call from my brother saying that she was declining faster than expected, and that the hospice nurse was giving Mom about a week. So, I booked a one-way flight and headed north.

I arrived at 3:00 a.m. Everyone was asleep so I did my best to be quiet as I slipped into my mom's room on Monday, February 26th to get a blanket in the corner where I knew she kept her extras. Of course, I bumped the wall, and she woke saying, "Who's there?"

"It's me, Mom," I responded.

"Who?"

"It's Brenda, Mom. Sorry I woke You."

"Oh, Hi Sis, what time is it?"

"It's three in the morning, Mom. I didn't mean to wake you!"

"Oh baby, you must be exhausted. Why don't you climb into bed with me and get some rest?"

So, I did just that. I stayed right there most of the time. I didn't get a lot of rest, but I was grateful to be by her side.

I spent my time reading what I knew to be some of her favorite scriptures out loud and singing, sometimes through tears, her favorite songs. I told her I was going to pray out loud and she could agree with me. One of the prayers I prayed was on behalf of my oldest son who had recently lost a big client and so had lost some of his income.

My mom was in and out of consciousness during most of that first day. Once she woke saying, "It's good that I am going to heaven so I can see those who have gone before me." I smiled and told her to say Hi to Grandma, Grandpa, and Aunt Bess for me.

Another time, she woke and began to instruct me to go find her purse and get her card and go to the bank and get some money because "Patrick needs help." I can't relate that part of the story without fighting back tears. Even on her death bed, she was looking for ways to help someone else. Later that same day, one of my uncles came to visit. Mom was aware enough to agree together with me and my uncle as we prayed for his health, nodding her head, and saying "Amen."

All this reflected Mom's heart and encouraged me through the last day of her life. Even though she was seemingly out of it, she could hear me and others that came along to pay their respects.

Mom even displayed her consideration for me and my brother by planning her own funeral years in advance. She had three songs picked out and indicated who she wanted to do the service. Probably ten years ago she told me that she had a life insurance policy. "It's enough to bury me but not much else," she said with a chuckle.

My favorite part of her plan was something she wanted on the pamphlet they always give out for folks to remember the person who has passed. Mom was a retired schoolteacher and many of her former students attended her funeral. She had written "Class is dismissed. The teacher has gone home." ☺ I just love that! As my pastor would say, she's where she's lived her life to be.

Mom even impressed the Hospice nurse by her responses. The nurse told me that when she told my mom that she probably had only a week left, my mom's response was "Yippee!" with her finger in the air and a bright smile on l her face.

"I have been doing this for 30 years and I have never had that response." Said the nurse as she told me this story.

Overall, I am so grateful for God's mercy. On Mom's last day she was seemingly unaware and certainly at peace. I was by her side. I woke to check on her and found her gone at 12:45 a.m. on leap day. Somebody said she "Leapt into heaven." ☺The definition of leapt is to jump or spring a long way, to a great height, or with great force. Also, to jump across or over. She would have loved that!

So, she was my hero all my life to her last day. Setting the best example. How many people have you heard of who approached their death with such grace and peace? For the last couple years Mom had lost her ability to sing due to a warble in her voice. The Lord comforted my heart when He reminded me that she is now able to sing her praises full volume with her voice fully restored. Oh, how she loved to sing.! I can just picture her up there giving the angels a run for their money. Thanks again Mom!

*Precious (important and no light matter) in the sight of the Lord is the death of His saints (His loving ones) Psalms 116:15 AMPC*

# ABOUT THE AUTHOR

The Author is a mother of three grown children and 7 grandchildren. She has been married for 38 years. She jokingly says she was practically born in the church nursery. She went to Christian school for most of her school years. She has been a professional secretary, a stay-at-home mother, and an assistant teacher / tutor, to name a few of her roles in life. Married to a military man, she has lived in many locations throughout the United States as well as a three-year tour in Italy.

Mrs. Ferry draws from a rich Godly heritage. Growing up in a small town in Iowa, she had her godly mother, who lived an exemplary life of trusting God. She had a prayer-warrior grandmother who talked of seeing angels and having visions. From these godly women and her own experiences, she has learned the value of trusting in her God and resting in His Peace. She has a passion for sharing with others in hopes of helping them find God's wonderful Peace as well.

Printed in the United States
by Baker & Taylor Publisher Services